$1 BILLION
2 BROTHERS
3 EXITS
200+ LESSONS

CATCH
OF THE
DECADE

HOW TO LAUNCH, BUILD
AND SELL A DIGITAL BUSINESS

GABBY LEIBOVICH + HEZI LEIBOVICH

WILEY

First published in 2021 by John Wiley & Sons Australia, Ltd
42 McDougall St, Milton Qld 4064
Office also in Melbourne

Typeset in ITC Giovanni Std 11pt/15pt

ISBN: 978-0-730-38849-4

A catalogue record for this
book is available from the
National Library of Australia

Cover design by Wiley

Cover and 'Catches' background image © greoli/Shutterstock

Back Cover Photo: © Erin Jonasson / Fairfax Media

Scooter image on p20 by Niran Kasri from Pixabay

10 9 8 7 6 5 4 3 2 1

Disclaimer
The material in this publication is of the nature of general comment only, and does not represent professional advice. It is not intended to provide specific guidance for particular circumstances and it should not be relied on as the basis for any decision to take action or not take action on any matter which it covers. Readers should obtain professional advice where appropriate, before making any such decision. To the maximum extent permitted by law, the authors and publisher disclaim all responsibility and liability to any person, arising directly or indirectly from any person taking or not taking action based on the information in this publication.

This book is dedicated to our supportive and amazing wives,
Amanda and Lina; and our children, Liron, Shira,
Miri, Daniel, Meital and Liam.

Dream big and believe anything is possible.

* * * * * *

One hundred per cent of our profits from this book
go to the following charities:

Good360.org

secondbite.org

Please support them, they do a good job!

Check out our book website for more great photos, videos, lessons and blogs:

catchofthedecade.com

CONTENTS

INTRODUCTION

How do two immigrant brothers with no money, limited industry knowledge, amateur technical skills and strong accents (that hasn't changed much ...) build some of Australia's most successful digital businesses with a combined exit valued at more than $1 billion?

It's a good question. We get asked it a lot, which is why we wrote this book.

You won't know our names and you probably won't recognise our faces, but you'll almost certainly know some of the brands we built, sold and/or merged for more than $1 billion after just 13 years in business.

Here are just a few of them:

- *Catchoftheday:* Australia's most popular shopping site
- *EatNow/Menulog:* an app that revolutionised the food delivery business
- *Scoopon:* a major disruptor in the services and entertainment sector
- *Luxury Escapes:* a travel deal site that made luxury travel affordable for all.

How did we build these brands, and, more importantly, how did we sell them for such a huge amount? Not by watching midday TV, working a nine-to-five job or borrowing money from a rich uncle to 'give things a go'. We built these brands with our bare hands, doing everything ourselves (surrounded by great people, of course) and doing it the hard way.

But what does 'doing it the hard way' even mean?

It means:

- getting up at dawn in the freezing cold to set up a market stall in Wantirna (in suburban Melbourne) to sell imperfect clothes, while all our mates were sleeping off their hangovers from the night before

- driving around the industrial sites of Melbourne in a beaten-up, Mitsubishi one-tonne van, cold-calling hard-nosed suppliers to try to source our 'catch of the day', hoping those suppliers wouldn't notice we were selling their stuff online

- hauling the stock back to our warehouse, unpacking it, photographing it, writing ads, answering customer emails, building online sites, packing up goods and schlepping them to the post office … every … single … day. (A quick 'Hi!' to Kate and Kevin from Caulfield post office. We saw more of them than we did our best friends at the time.)

As the Catch business grew, a typical day for us would look something like this: upon waking, we'd check our emails. We'd drive to the office, be at our desks by 8 am, solve the problems from the night before (we were a 24/7 business), attend a supplier meeting at 9 am, juggle a thousand different balls and decisions throughout the morning, eat a hurried lunch at our desk, have more meetings with suppliers in the afternoon, head home at 8 pm, have a quick dinner, kiss the kids, say hello to our wives, hit the desk for another few hours, answer more emails, get to bed around 1 am and then get up and do it all again the next day. You could say we 'bootstrapped' it.

LOOKING BACK, BOOTSTRAPPING WAS THE ONLY WAY WE COULD DO IT.

We had no money, no experience and no contacts, so doing it ourselves was the only option. And besides, no-one had ever built a business like this before, so we had no roadmap to follow. But we did it, and we're here to share the stories and lessons we learned along the way so you can hopefully take a few shortcuts and get to where you're going faster.

We want to make your journey to success as easy as possible so we're sharing much of what we've learned with you. We've held nothing back.

In this book you'll find:

- more than 200 bite-sized nuggets of wisdom called 'Catches', which you'll find at the end of each of the three parts of this book

- 21 longer-style 'lessons', which are dotted throughout the book

- snippets of emails and phone scripts that helped us build this business from the ground up

- numbers and more numbers: revenue, profits, products sold and much more

- screenshots of the early advertisements and websites that helped us launch our businesses

- a raft of 'live' examples of materials you can use and be inspired by.

The businesses we built

Before launching into part I of the book, we thought we'd give you a bit of background on the businesses we built, along with a business timeline to put our Catch story into perspective.

Fast facts

Catchoftheday was launched in October 2006. From humble beginnings of selling just one deal a day, by 2010 it had become Australia's most visited online shopping site. In 2017, the site added a marketplace capability in order to compete with eBay and Amazon, and it was rebranded to become Catch.com.au. In August 2019, Catch.com.au was sold for $230 million to Wesfarmers, which owns some of Australia's leading retailers: Bunnings, Kmart, Target and Officeworks. Today, Catch employs more than 500 staff and has yearly revenues exceeding $600 million.

Scoopon was launched in April 2010 and had a similar 'deal of the day' concept to Catchoftheday but sold discounted coupons for services and travel. Scoopon revolutionised the way businesses such as restaurants, hairdressers and masseurs marketed their services. In 2012, Scoopon Travel was launched, offering travel discounts on accommodation, tours and flights. We launched five-star luxury travel website Bon Voyage not long after, and in late 2017 both Scoopon Travel and Bon Voyage were acquired by leading travel deal site Luxury Escapes.

Grocery Run was launched in September 2011 and became part of the combined Catch Group*. It pioneered the concept of selling grocery items online and paved the way for the giants of supermarket retailing to launch their e-commerce sites.

---

* The Catch Group (and sometimes simply 'Catch') is a loose term we used to describe the growing clutch of businesses that we were launching. It is not a legal entity but a quick way of referring to our collective businesses.

Mumgo was launched in July 2012 with the slogan, 'Where mums go', with the aim of entering the burgeoning kids' and baby markets. Mumgo was later integrated back into the Catch.com.au website.

EAT NOW   MENULOG

EatNow was launched in October 2012 as a food ordering app. EatNow was one of the original disruptors that introduced the food home delivery concept to Australia, paving the way for Uber Eats and Deliveroo to enter Australia. In early 2015 EatNow merged with market leader **Menulog**, which in May 2015 was acquired by the UK conglomerate Just Eat for $855 million.

LUXURYESCAPES

Luxury Escapes is a travel business founded by Adam Schwab and Jeremy Same. While we didn't build this amazing business, in 2017 we became part owners after we merged our two travel businesses, Bon Voyage and Scoopon Travel with Luxury Escapes.

The Catch timeline

2004

	Ran independent eBay businesses from our respective garages

2006

June	Collaborated to launch DailyDeals.com.au
October	Launched Catchoftheday.com.au with five employees

2008

September	Moved Catchoftheday operations to Springvale warehouse

2010

April	Launched Scoopon
September	Moved Catchoftheday into combined office and warehouse in Moorabbin

2011

May	Tiger Global acquired a 40 per cent stake in the Catchoftheday business for $80 million
August	Moved into combined office and warehouse in Braeside
September	Launched Grocery Run

2012

July	Launched Mumgo
July	Acquired Vinomofo
November	Leased a warehouse at Truganina

2014

October	Completed the $20 million automation of the Truganina warehouse and fulfilment process

2015

January	Announced merger of Menulog and EatNow
May	Announced sale of Menulog/EatNow
June	Launched Club Catch

2016

July	Catchoftheday bought back the 40 per cent stake from Tiger Global to become a 100 per cent privately owned company again

2017

June	Rebranded Catchoftheday as Catch.com.au and launched the Catch Marketplace
July	Launched Bon Voyage
August	Acquired Pumpkin Patch
December	Sold Scoopon to Lux Group
	Acquired Brands Exclusive and The Home
	Merged Bon Voyage and Scoopon Travel with Luxury Escapes

2018

February	Launched Catch Connect

2019

August	Sold Catch.com.au to Wesfarmers for $230 million

The early days! We had no idea the business would grow to be so big. We were just having fun, playing with computers.
Source: © Michael Clayton-Jones / Fairfax Media

ESTABLISHED
2006

PART 1
Getting started

CHAPTER 1
How it all began

Success came to us late. We were in our thirties when we hit on the idea for Catchoftheday, but before that we worked hard at building shitty little businesses that never seemed to take hold. We had no idea that all those shitty little businesses were small steps towards building much bigger, more successful businesses—some of which would disrupt several industries in the Australian market and shake the retail sector to its core.

If you haven't succeeded yet, don't give up

We started our retail 'careers' selling at the markets, the best training ground for commerce you can get. That experience helped us develop a pretty thick skin, which served us well and inured us to all manner of insults and injuries. Starting high school in Australia as teenagers with weird accents, limited English and an aversion to AFL toughened us up even more. But in hindsight, being outsiders made us who we are today.

Raised on hummus and chutzpah*

Our father, Shlomo (Aaron) immigrated to Israel from Romania as a child, and our mum Editha (Edith) was an immigrant from the Ukraine. They met, got married, had three kids—Gabby, the eldest; Einat, our sister; and Hezi—and raised us in Nahariya, a beautiful seaside town in Israel. Our birthplace holds a very special place in our hearts. It was a city where everyone knew and cared for one another. Israel is the home of Jewish immigrants from all parts of the world and, as such, we got to share the best and worst moments of growing up in this war-affected region with friends and neighbours from many cultures and countries: Spain, Morocco, Romania, Poland, Iraq, Russia, Iran and more.

Our community was colourful, vibrant and full of love, laughter and noise. Every family in our apartment block had an average of four kids, and dozens of families shared a play area the size of an Aussie backyard. After walking to school in the mornings (six days a week, not five as is the norm in Australia), the afternoons would be filled with soccer, surfing and wandering the streets hanging out with our friends until it was time to go to bed. We didn't have any devices or internet and we were the better for it. We often tell our kids that we had the best childhood ever, surrounded by friends, love and great weather.

All the parents were out working hard to support the families, so we kids had no option but to grow up fast, fend for ourselves and face life head on. Growing up in this tightknit neighbourhood taught us how to accept people from all cultures, share what we

---

* Chutzpah has no equivalent in the English language, but in Hebrew it means arrogant, audacious and brazen. In a business sense it means finding an undiplomatic and creative way of getting things done.

had and be tolerant of other points of view: all valuable life skills that have served us well ever since.

Our childhood sounds idyllic, and it truly was, but it certainly wasn't an average childhood. The closest most Australian kids get to experiencing war is playing video games such as *World of Warcraft* or *Call of Duty*. For us, however, war was real. During the conflict with Lebanon in 1982, our city, being the northernmost city on the Mediterranean, was the main target for rocket missiles into Israel. We'll never forget huddling in our houses or shelters during war times, and hearing the non-stop whistles of rockets falling all around us. *Wheeeeeee Boom! Wheeeeeee Boom!*

When the rockets stopped, all the kids in the neighbourhood would continue life as if nothing had happened, except for one popular local challenge. We'd all run around to see who could find the largest piece of missile shrapnel and show it off to our family and friends. (You could say we did 'show and tell' a little differently in Israel.) Every kid in the neighbourhood had a prized collection of shrapnel in their bedroom. We kept ours on the top of a bookshelf, next to Gabby's poster of Samantha Fox and our 34-centimetre black-and-white Metz TV.

Growing up during a war-torn period like this made us impervious to most forms of fear and forced us to make a decision. Do we let these situations scare us and stop us from living life? Or do we find a way to overcome them and turn them to our advantage? We chose the latter.

As a result, things that scared others never really scared us. After all, when you've had bombs exploding outside your front door, what is there left to be fearful of? A customer saying, 'I won't buy your product'; a journalist saying, 'I can't cover your story'; a supplier saying, 'We won't let you sell our products'? Meh.

The third door

Our dad, who showed us what persistence really means, said to us, 'There's the front door, the back door, and then there's the third door'. That was the door you took when all the others were shut. Being poor immigrants (we moved to Australia because our parents were looking for a better life) this third door was often the only one open to us. His strong example of how to push through the doors that were closed has stayed with us ever since.

> 'THERE'S THE FRONT DOOR, THE BACK DOOR, AND THEN THERE'S THE THIRD DOOR'.

This 'no fear' attitude paid dividends, especially in the early Catch days when we and our small team were working hard to get things done and make a noise. It also helped us get noticed by everyone who mattered: the customers, the suppliers and the media. The support of all three created the magic that enabled Catch (and all our other businesses) to become the ferocious disruptors that went on to fight the giants (some of them dinosaurs!) of Australian retail.

It all started at the dinner table

Our parents were unusual in that they exposed us to entrepreneurial thinking from a very early age. In other words, we talked about 'how to make money' a lot. In fact, at dinner it was our favourite topic. Their attitude? Don't focus on saving money. Find ways to make money. Their advice gave us a high appetite for risk, and cultivated within us a mentality of innovation and creativity—all crucial skills for being an entrepreneur.

Our father was an electronics engineer who worked multiple jobs to support the family. In Israel he worked for the Department of Defence, and when we moved to Australia he ran a series of electronic stores and had a market stall at Croydon in the outer south-eastern suburbs of Melbourne. He was an old-fashioned kind of entrepreneur, the kind who could spot an opportunity wherever he went. For example, growing up in Israel, he discovered that changing his car over was a quick and easy way to earn a buck. His modus operandi was to buy a second-hand car at a good price (his favourite was the Peugeot Model 404, mainly because it was the taxi driver's car of choice) and on-sell it for a higher price.

Dad's business model was pretty basic: he didn't buy a new car or add new features, he just searched high and low for a good deal (in the pre-internet days, this was really hard work) by driving around the country to locate the best cars at the lowest prices. He'd then add value by giving the car a quick repair, a spit and polish, and then resell it for a profit.

We've followed this same 'business model' ever since and we can attribute much of our success to it. We learned a valuable lesson early on: you make your money when you buy the goods, not when you sell them. If you buy low, selling the product is easy.

Building the family business

Being brothers, and sharing a room for 16 years growing up, we knew each other well, and could rely on each other to do the right thing. This trust enabled us to build the Catch business together but work on separate things, thereby doubling our output. We often worked in separate locations on different parts of the business, so we sometimes didn't even know exact details about what the other was doing. But we always knew we were there for each other and had each other's back, no matter what.

We mostly speak as one throughout this book, but occasionally we'll break out and tell you an individual story. To get started, here's an honest, in-your-face appraisal of what we think of each other because, we know each other best.

Gabby

Hezi and I are quite different. He's the quieter (younger) one. Anyone who knows him knows he loves building things and solving problems: if he had become a watchmaker he would have really enjoyed tinkering with the mechanism rather than the hands and alarm. He loves to challenge the norm and often says, 'surely there is a better way of doing things!' For example, a pizza shop owner getting Hezi's order wrong three times in a row over the phone ultimately led to the creation of EatNow, which was one of our most successful ventures. Even growing up, he was so annoyed by having to get up from the computer to shut the bedroom door, he built a remote door opener so he could open or close it just by pressing a button. He's a very innovative kind of guy.

Hezi

Gabby's the talkative one, the cheeky one, the provocateur. Like all great entrepreneurs, Gabby is highly curious about everything, asks great questions and puts people at ease very quickly. He takes a genuine interest in those around him and those who work with him. People love working with him, and want to go the extra mile for him. You can't make people care about the company they work for, but Gabby does, and as a result he's built a long-serving and loyal team. He humbly calls himself 'just a buyer' but he's much more than that. He has an eye for detail, is blindingly quick with figures (he gave me a quick $50 to write all this ...) and is very humorous—all of which enables him to deal with a multitude of personalities up and down the business hierarchy.

Gabby

Hezi is talented at inventing new and innovative business concepts and has a strong intuition about which ideas to pursue and which ones to leave alone. He thrives on taking on new challenges, building a business model and then hitting the pavement to see if it works. He hates wasting money, so he'll pursue the idea on his own to check if the business model stands up to scrutiny before recruiting and building new teams. For example, when testing the Scoopon concept, he visited more than 100 businesses across Melbourne—car washes, masseuses and the like—and took with him an A3 sheet of paper of a draft Scoopon website homepage, which he used to show the business owners how the concept worked in order to discover what kind of commission they would accept. He even called himself 'Harry' because the Catch brand was well known and he didn't want to get preferential treatment. In every business, he always surveyed the land before he sent in soldiers. That's something I've always respected in a great entrepreneur.

Hezi

Gabby does the public speaking, and the bragging. He's been the face of the company since we began, and has represented us in all the TV and newspaper interviews. At the beginning he hated public speaking, but when you see him on stage, you can see he's a natural performer, and as time went on, he grew to love it and became brilliant at it, which is just as well because every start-up needs a front person who can spruik the business.

Some people have the 'star' factor and some don't. Gabby has it in spades (another $50 for this one!). His sense of style, showmanship and storytelling are second to none, and while these attributes come to him with ease, he supplements that natural skill with hard work. Who else could come up with lines like these:

We sell people shit they don't need at prices they can't resist.

We never spent a cent on marketing and advertising.

We're Australia Post's No. 1 client.

WE SELL PEOPLE SHIT THEY DON'T NEED AT PRICES THEY CAN'T RESIST.

That last one worked a treat. We asked Australia Post if it was true and they never denied it, so Gabby figured he may as well keep saying it. He's always had the gift of the Gab. Could our parents have chosen a better name for him? I think not. That kind of 'there-are-no-rules' and 'if-there-are-they're-made-to-be-broken' school of business enabled us to become the number-one most popular shopping site in Australia. (That claim, by the way, is true. Hitwise told us so.)

Gabby

Hezi loves fast take-offs, speed and the adrenaline and disruption of launching a start-up. Usually, after a few years, when the plane reaches altitude and the crew is well positioned to see the journey through, he ventures off looking for a new endeavour and just loves to do it all over again, adding layers of value to each business he builds.

What many may not know is that Hezi is a trained chiropractor. Unwilling and, quite frankly, unable to work for anyone else—we'd never worked for anyone but our dad—he set up a chiro clinic and used a 'free spinal check' to recruit new patients in shopping centres, working 10-hour days on the floor. He also owes a lot to good old Bert Newton, who unknowingly gave him a hand in launching his business ... but more on that later.

Hezi

Gabby is a mad soccer fan, has huge reserves of chutzpah and uses that quality daily to get what he wants. His passion, madness and love for soccer intersected in 2002, when he secretly asked the Leeds soccer team to host his wedding on the soccer pitch at Melbourne's (now) Marvel Stadium—and they agreed! He got married in front of 25000 screaming soccer fans (and one surprised bride) and it didn't cost him a cent. That's Gabby all over. (You can check the wedding out on YouTube: 'Gabby Leeds Wedding'.)

It seems redundant to say that his chutzpah, which at times was expressed by kicking doors, became a real asset in the early days of Catch, when most brands would tell us, 'We don't sell to online stores'. As strange as it may seem now, finding good deals back then was hard. It was Gabby's potent mixture of zeal and charm that convinced them to sell their excess stock to him, which was a crucial and defining characteristic for building a successful, powerful Catch.

Having shared a room with him growing up, I can say with certainty that Gabby is one of the craziest guys I've ever met, but he's my crazy brother and I love him.

Gabby: The epitome of chutzpah! Asking the Leeds soccer team if I can get married on the pitch at half time during their game at Marvel Stadium. My poor wife! She deserves a medal.

Gabby

Hezi's work ethic is prodigious. We don't take days off, are always 'on' and there is never a 'wrong' time to talk about the business. It is not uncommon for Hezi to send and answer emails at 3 am, even now. We have had a successful working relationship for all these years because we each have our own 'unofficial' roles in the business. For example, after it was proposed we should build a brand-new, $20 million, 23 000 m² warehouse (which is about the size of the MCG!), Hezi approved the proposal within minutes with a WhatsApp message that said, 'Sounds good!'. He trusted me sufficiently without needing to second guess. Similarly, after four years at Catch, when Hezi went off to start Scoopon and EatNow, I approved it with a message saying, 'Cool!'

This trust extended to the day-to-day operations too. For example, Hezi is great at understanding the digital complexities of UX, UI, SEO and SEM*. To me it's just a big WTF**! He, on the other hand has an allergy to some of the things I love, like writing the copy for billboards and newspaper ads. He lets me do my thing, and I let him do his.

This trust has been fundamental to our success. It doesn't matter if we are making a $2000 decision, or a $20 million decision, we trust each other to do the right thing by the business.

He's my younger brother, he knows me better than anyone and I love him.

---

* UX (user experience), UI (user interface), SEO (search engine optimisation), SEM (search engine marketing).
** WTF: You may want to look that up yourself.

Working weekends at the market

Not long after arriving in Australia in 1986, our parents set up a stall selling stuff at Croydon market. While our neighbours went to the beach on a Sunday, the Leibovich family went to work. It wasn't optional. We all had to go.

As soon as Gabby turned 18 (Hezi was 12 at the time) and got his licence and his Holden Gemini, we struck out on our own and set up another stall at Wantirna market. We'd arrive at the Wantirna market car park at 4 am on a Sunday to secure our place in the car park queue. Sometimes we'd even sleep in the car overnight to ensure we were in a good position when the doors opened. Then, as now, location is everything. At 8 am they'd let us in and as soon as the gates opened, we'd race to get the best spot.

> **GABBY WOULD SHAMELESSLY JUMP ON THE TABLE AND SPRUIK AT THE TOP OF HIS VOICE TO GET US NOTICED. HE TURNED THE STALL INTO A SHOW.**

We sold clearance apparel that we managed to source from a factory in Clayton (thank you Mr Roitman for giving us our first break!). On our first day, we made $700 in five hours. Not bad for a couple of kids. We packed up and went home early as we'd sold out of everything.

But there was a reason for that success. Other than our great merchandise, we found a way to increase our chances of success. We put our individual talents to work. Gabby would shamelessly jump on the table and spruik at the top of his voice to get us noticed. He turned the stall into a show. As the crowd gathered to see what the hell was going on, Hezi would pitch the benefits of owning a beautiful $2 Australiana T-shirt with a picture of an echidna or emu on it, and why everyone in the family should own one as well. We also set up a very efficient bagging and payment process, so it ran like clockwork. We were a great double act.

The challenge of working in any market—online or offline—is that sometimes all the stallholders sell the same thing: row after row of it. It's crucial to have a point of difference. The great thing is that you don't always have to reinvent the wheel. It's okay to be inspired elsewhere and apply it to your own circumstances. One of the more memorable vendors we recall from our time selling at the market was a guy called Jonno, an older guy who'd been working the markets for years. He'd stand up on the back of his truck, speak into a crackly hand-held microphone, hold up one product at a time, and work the crowd into a fever on the premise he only had a few in stock and once the product was gone, it was gone. The crowd would fight to give him their money and his wife would move around, pocketing the cash as quickly as she could. They sold so much they hired someone to hold open the bags so his wife could stuff the product in and move on to the next person.

This concept of focusing on one item at a time, within a limited time span, and spruiking it loudly to the world, must have seeped into our subconscious because those three principles formed the basis of what Catchoftheday would become.

The cut and thrust of the markets was our introduction to running our own retail business, and after a while we became quite good at the basics of the retail trade. What's more, we could see a direct correlation between our efforts and our earnings, and we loved every moment of it! We've taken many lessons from those market days and applied them to our business. Buying, pricing, selling, haggling—it's all part of the act. We've been 'playing' at it since we were kids. It's in our DNA. It's who we are.

Something has to change

 Gabby

In the mid-1990s, a few years after the markets, our family started a business called Panasales, a factory outlet of heavily discounted electronic appliances. Hezi and our sister Einat worked there on weekends and I worked there full time. It was always busy, noisy and filled with young men smelling of Lynx. This was a great learning period in my life, and I will be forever thankful for my years working in 'retail land'. It was a school for entrepreneurs unlike any other. Working on the floor, I was able to see up close what made the customer tick, and it helped me become a better salesman. I was also able to get close to the suppliers, and that exposure taught me the secrets of buying well, which is the essence of being a successful retailer.

Working on the floor is also where I developed my love of marketing. One of my jobs was to create the ads for the store. I wrote the copy, developed the offer, devised the tag lines and negotiated the rates with the media. We'd advertise every Thursday in *The Age*'s 'Green Guide', and knew how good the ad was by the number of phone calls we received the next day. I did my homework to ensure our pricing was the best in the market. I'd visit all our competitors, including JB Hi-Fi, Good Guys, Harvey Norman and Myer, take notes, compare prices and create comparison ads that really made the phone ring. This is what they looked like:

Sharp TV, Model XYZ

Myer $1099   JB Hi-Fi $999   Panasales $749

This pricing data is all now available online of course, but back then I had to research it manually and, in the process, learned a lot about how to keep an eye on competitors.

At this point, I was 33 years old, working in a family business, and living in a tiny unit in Caulfield. Other than my supportive wife and baby daughter, I have to be honest and say that there wasn't much excitement in my life. I basically sold electronics all day, came home, and that was it. I knew the business could expand and go to greater heights. There's no question Panasales was one of the busiest, most popular electronic stores in Melbourne, maybe Australia. It was an institution. Problem was, there was only one store, and it was in suburban Melbourne. Scaling it the traditional way meant opening new premises in different locations, and that wasn't cheap, or easy. Online shopping was not on the cards ... yet.

'Free spinal check': three words I never want to hear again

 Hezi

When I finished high school, I wanted to be a chiro. I enrolled in a course, but it was so expensive I had to find a way to pay it off. After a few successful print runs of selling T-shirts to chiro students, and a few other similar types of 'lemonade stand' moments (which were fun but were never going to make a dent in my student loan), I felt like I had to come up with a more lucrative idea. By that time, I had established a small network of chiropractors who I befriended and circled as future mentors or employers. One day, I asked a few of them what they most wanted for their chiro practice. In unison, they all said 'more customers'.

My brain started ticking and I came up with an idea. I struck up a deal with one of those chiropractors to generate new customers for their clinic and get paid based on performance. Here was the model: I would offer a basic free spinal check (a 'freemium' model in today's terminology) to passers-by at a shopping centre, and if there was a need and they wanted a more comprehensive assessment, like x-rays or a proper spinal analysis, I would offer them a discounted voucher that would entitle them to $160 worth of chiro services for just $45. The customer got a good deal; the chiro acquired a new customer, and I got to keep the $45 for my efforts. A triple win.

With this business underway, I was now making more money than ever before and I was working for myself, both of which were important to me. On the downside, I was getting worn down. The process was laborious, time intensive and difficult to scale. I wanted to expand to other shopping centres and grow the business but it was hard to recruit for the role. Despite the job paying five times more than what my chiro student friends were making at their pub jobs, they refused to embarrass themselves by standing at the shopping centre spruiking a chiro service to those walking by. I understood their hesitation. It takes a certain type of humility to be able to stand in a shopping centre for 10 hours a day and have nine out of 10 people walk by and ignore you. In my mind, every person who said 'no' to me or ignored me was basically saying, 'I hate you'. I know that's not true, but that's how it felt. That's part of the sales process and now I'm used to it, but in those early days, when I was just getting started, that kind of treatment really stung. I've never forgotten it. I have enormous empathy for sales people. They are the heart of any organisation and determine if it succeeds or not.

As I couldn't be in two places at the same time and was restricted to operating one stand at a time, the only way to go to the next level was to open a stand at a bigger venue. One year, I hired a large stand at the Melbourne Home Show in the Exhibition Centre. It was extremely busy and when you have a sign offering something for 'free', the line of people is often 20 metres long. I was talking non-stop from 10 am to 10 pm for 10 days, checking thousands of spines and getting exhausted.

At one point I was so tired I almost passed out, so I closed the stand for 15 minutes and went for a walk to get some fresh air. On my way back to the stand I noticed a massive crowd gathered around a man standing on a chair shouting into a microphone.

His stall was a quarter the size of mine, but 50 people were hanging on his every word. What was he spruiking? ... A Car Baby. A *what?* Exactly. It was an early version of a mobile phone hands-free device. The scene instantly took me back to my days at the market when Jonno stood on the back of his truck and hawked his wares.

The crazy thing, though, was this guy made more in 15 minutes than I had made all day. We were both selling $50 products, but there were some crucial differences. The Car Baby was an easy product to understand and had wide appeal; he sold only one version of the product; and because he was selling to one big group, he could reach more people more quickly. He was doing everything I should have been doing but wasn't, and couldn't.

The light bulb went on. My business model was fatally flawed. I had picked the wrong product to spruik. Selling my service was hard, slow, needed skill and education, took a lot of convincing and couldn't scale. Other than that, it was great!

I needed to change my business model, and, more importantly, I needed to change what I sold. I needed to sell the Car Baby.

The 'can't fail' idea

 Gabby

The 2002 FIFA World Cup in Japan/South Korea was coming up and I thought there had to be a marketing opportunity somewhere here. So, I did some research to see what I could sell. I discovered a product in China that I was sure would be my ticket to success: the MobiBall. Picture it: an oversized, plush soccer ball with a dock on the top for your mobile phone. When a call comes in, the phone bounces and sings 'Olé! Olé, Olé!' The greatest thing since sliced bread, right? Who wouldn't want one?

I flew to Hong Kong with my wife Amanda to pick up the product and play the big-shot businessman. I dropped my life savings on buying 3000 of these balls to import to Australia. I also spent $8000 on a van to deliver the MobiBall to the hordes of demanding customers who were sure to buy it. I rented a stand at Melbourne's Moomba Festival and stood there with Amanda from dawn to dusk over four long days trying to sell my amazing new product to anyone who walked by. I think we sold about twenty balls. They were the four most embarrassing days of my life. I had the balloon clown on one side of my stand, the Dagwood dog seller on the other and they both sold more than I did. The disdain on people's faces as they walked past me is etched in my mind. I'll never forget that experience.

Clearly the only person who thought the MobiBall was a good idea was me. What a waste of time! I learned two lessons that day. Don't let your passion for a product cloud your commercial judgement, and sell something that is easy for the customer to understand. The MobiBall failed on both counts. That 'can't fail' idea cost me $30 000, half my life savings at the time. An expensive, but valuable experience. Every entrepreneur has to learn these lessons at some stage. I'm just glad I learned them when I was young. Those 3000 MobiBalls went into the bin, but my entrepreneurial dreams did not. I was still keen to do something and put my hard-won knowledge to good use. I just didn't know what.

(A big shout out to my wife Amanda. She deserves a medal for sticking by this crazy entrepreneur for so many years. I think I'll take her to the next World Cup for our wedding anniversary. She doesn't know that yet but she's going to love it.)

 Hezi

By 2004 I had moved on from selling chiro vouchers and was selling Car Babies at my shopping centre stall when I noticed a young guy loitering around my stall. He said, 'I work for the advertising agency that creates advertorials for Bert Newton's morning TV show. Those Car Babies you have there would sell like hotcakes.'

His price for the advertising spot was way out of my budget (which was zero) but he wouldn't take 'no' for an answer. The kid was either new, desperate, a little bit crazy or a blend of all three. He made his final offer. 'Tell you what, how about we split the media fee? I pay half, you pay half?'

I didn't have the money, I didn't watch Bert Newton, I didn't even watch morning TV, but I was so tired of standing there waiting for customers to come along, I was willing to try anything.

I took him up on his offer and flew into action. I wrote, shot and produced the TV commercial. I found a call centre that could take the orders over the phone, designed the packaging, sourced the products from China, wrote the script, found a presenter to spruik the TV ad, and ticked all the boxes needed to pull it all together. To be honest, I didn't have a lot of faith in this working at all, but since I'd paid for everything, I was going to give it my best shot.

Leading up to the ad appearing, I was a nervous wreck. I couldn't sleep. I couldn't eat. I'd invested my life savings into this. Everything I had was riding on this one ad. It had to work. Long story short, the ad was a smash. With one four-minute ad, I sold 1600 Car Babies. Compared to standing around for a full day at a shopping centre selling 40 units, this was a game changer; this was scalable.

Believe it or not, within a year, I was spending $5 million on media space alone spruiking all kinds of 'As Seen on TV' gadgets. That young guy who went 50/50 on the media fee with me? He got the commission. Not a bad payday for hanging around my shopping stall and asking a question or two. It just goes to show: it pays to ask. I also learned that day that it pays to say 'yes' to an opportunity, even if you don't know what the next step is.

The second product we sold on TV was electric scooters. We also sold them at the shopping centre and direct from the warehouse. They were so popular, we had 50 people lined up outside the warehouse every Saturday wanting to buy one. It was going gangbusters but a few days out from Christmas, disaster struck. The Victorian government, with no prior announcement or consultation with the industry, decided to ban the sale of electric scooters—'for safety reasons', they said, or something like that. With one fell swoop of a politician's pen, the product I had been successfully selling was banned. If I'd just had a few scooters sitting in the shop, it wouldn't have been so bad. But I had 12 huge containers of scooters from China sitting on the dock in Port Melbourne, waiting to be unpacked.

As if that ban wasn't bad enough, the government mandated that anyone who had purchased one could return it for a full refund. Customers turned up with trashed scooters that looked like they'd completed the Dakar Rally, wanting a refund, and I gave them one. It was the right thing to do, but it nearly bankrupted me*. Fortunately, the ban didn't extend to New South Wales, so I was able to offload the stock way below cost to an online retailer based in Sydney, Paul Greenberg of Deals Direct. The damage to the business was devastating. I'd worked non-stop for years and now here I was, 30 years old with not much to show for it, staring down another cold, dark, shitty Melbourne winter. There was only one solution. I had to get away. I had to have a sea change. I had to go to Queensland.

A little website called eBay

 Gabby

One day, back at Panasales, a customer showed me a little website called eBay. It got me thinking: if people without any

---

* Have you noticed that every big city has worked out that scooters are actually a good thing? Timing is everything.

sales experience could sell random items like rice cookers, quilts and DVD players, maybe I could too. What I liked most about the platform was that it cut out the intermediary. *You mean I don't have to talk to customers? Negotiate the price? Pay rent on a shop?* After 12 years of talking to people every day, the idea of the website doing the talking was very appealing.

What I loved most about it was that I could now sell to customers who were not in my suburb, I could sell for 24 hours a day, and unlike a physical retail store, I would incur zero set up costs. I got to work.

I chose a Wintal set-top box for $99 as my first listing, went to bed, woke up and saw I'd netted a profit of $200 while sleeping. I couldn't believe my eyes! If this was eBay, I wanted more of it. The best part? Suppliers were yet to spot the opportunity, so the market was wide open for people like me to take advantage of it. I started looking at everything through the lens of 'could this sell on eBay?' I got goose bumps thinking of all the suppliers I could source product from. Could it really be this easy?*

I jumped in my car and drove around to all our Panasales suppliers asking for stock to sell online. They didn't see me as a threat to their existing retailers so I had free rein to sell whatever they could give me. In reality, I was a direct competitor but because they'd never heard of eBay—*ePay?, eWay?*—I was able to get some traction very quickly. I flew completely under their radar. 'First mover advantage' is what they call it now. I called it being creative.

Many great brands at the time did not have any presence on eBay. This created an opportunity for people like me to introduce eBay shoppers to premium brands that weren't available online. Sunbeam was one of those brands but, being a high-end product, they were never going to permit me to sell their product online—or anywhere else for that matter. They wouldn't even give me a trading account.

---

* eBay back then was what department stores are today: empty, overpriced and understaffed.

But there's always that third door.

I did my research and discovered that Sunbeam had a factory outlet store in Maribyrnong, 11 kilometres north-west of Melbourne, and it was open to the general public. You beauty! I drove over in my trusty Mitsubishi one-tonne van, filled it with stock, took it home, photographed the stock, uploaded it to eBay, watched and waited … and sure enough, the sales rolled in. It's hard to believe now, but at that time, I was the only person selling Sunbeam online. I owned the market! My mission was to keep finding unique products just like that: products people wanted that couldn't be found anywhere online.

One memorable product that sold well in those early days was security safes. I'd buy them from Bunnings for $19, sell them for a huge profit, and make more money in a day than I'd made all week at Panasales. I still smile every time I walk past the safe aisle at Bunnings.

However, selling on eBay in those early days wasn't without its challenges. The downside of not having a lot of sellers online was that there weren't that many buyers online either. But all things considered, especially compared to now, selling online back then was a piece of cake. Those were the days!

The early incarnation of eBay was a topsy-turvy world. Items that you could buy for $20 in a brick-and-mortar store could sell for three or four times that at auction on eBay. People were willing to pay more for a host of different reasons. For some it was the thrill of the auction and the ability to access new products. For others it was the sheer convenience of having the products home delivered. For others again it was the novelty of buying online.

 ## Hezi

I called my online store DailyDeals.com.au. At the start, when sales were just trickling in, most people didn't trust online buying, and they certainly didn't like handing over a credit card, so a lot of the sales were paid for using cheques and postal money orders. I'd be lying if I didn't say that there were times I thought, 'Is this really worth the headache?'; however, my instinct was strong and it told me that this online thing was the way forward. It had to be. It just made sense.

While people didn't trust most online sites, there was one in particular they did trust. eBay. It had established itself as a trusted destination and was one place where customers freely handed over their credit card details. I decided to go where the customer was and set up an online store on eBay to take advantage of that trust.

So, it's late 2005. There's Gabby, building up his small eBay store from Melbourne. Meanwhile, Hezi is building up his small eBay store on the Gold Coast in Queensland. They were operating in parallel without realising it. So when Hezi returned to Melbourne, they decided that maybe they should pool their resources, and their websites, and work together. That small decision would turn out to have a massive impact.

CHAPTER 2

Working together

Once we had 'merged' our operations, we decided to take a risk and find an office/warehouse to have some space from where to operate our small business. Feeling very grown up, we signed a lease on a 180 m² warehouse at Roberna St in Moorabbin, just 13 minutes from home.

The business was still quite small, but it was moving in the right direction, getting more customers and making more money. Our first specialist 'hires' were two new immigrants with a background in e-commerce. Vijay, newly arrived from Malaysia, was brilliant at all things tech and IT; and Ferry, from Indonesia, was our computer programmer. We also hired some other guys to staff the warehouse, photograph the products, do the buying and manage customer service.

Looking back, we can see why we gravitated towards these guys. They were intelligent, hardworking allrounders with a passion to succeed, just like us. And the team just clicked. Our workplace was very egalitarian, more by chance than design. None of us knew what we were doing, none of us were experts at anything and none of us had better jobs than the other; we all just pitched in and did what needed to be done.

NONE OF US KNEW WHAT WE WERE DOING, NONE OF US WERE EXPERTS AT ANYTHING AND NONE OF US HAD BETTER JOBS THAN THE OTHER;

WE ALL JUST PITCHED IN AND DID WHAT NEEDED TO BE DONE.

- If a container landed from China, we all unloaded it together.

- If the warehouse had more orders than we could handle, someone would stop what they were doing and help out.

- If there were lots of emails, we all stayed as late as required to clear the mailbox.

- If a customer stepped into the store, any one of us would serve them.

You did what you had to do!

At this stage we had four separate arms to the business:

- the DailyDeals.com.au online department store

- the Daily Deals eBay store

- a direct-to-the-public warehouse shop (selling the same items we sold on eBay)

- 'As Seen on TV' television advertorials.

Those early days of 2006 were a massive learning curve for us. We were a true start-up, or as it was known then, a small business. We had no formal business plan, and had to learn everything on the run: from payroll, tax and accounting, to legal, HR and marketing. We did everything on the cheap—and we still do, if we can. Some call this being frugal. We call it being smart. We're amazed when we see start-ups spending money on EAs, PAs, VAs—Oy Vey!— and they haven't even made a sale, let alone a profit. We're even more amazed that some start-ups take three or four years, even a decade, to turn a profit.

We know there are lots of different business models for how start-ups can operate, and deferring profits to generate sales is a valid rationale, but as retailers with a background in markets, we felt then, and to some extent still feel, that a business is meant to make money from the start. Did we ever expect our start-up to get so big? Hardly. We were just trying to keep it afloat, pay the salaries and make the rent.

The day eBay shut us down

So, there we were, a bunch of guys operating mildly successful, but largely unheard-of, eBay stores out of our little office in suburban Melbourne, doing okay and living nice, simple lives. And it probably would have continued this way except that, for some inexplicable reason, eBay decided to suspend our trading account.

This action basically shut our business down overnight. We tried valiantly to get in touch with eBay to sort it out, but we couldn't find anyone to take our call. Their customer service team at the time sat in Canada and was only dealing with sophisticated larger sellers and ignored all our cries for help. We couldn't trade and were losing money, and customers, fast. This lasted for 15 days, and it began to bite. They eventually restored our account, but this stressful situation taught us three big lessons:

1. Don't put all your trust (or eggs) in one platform.

2. Own your own platform (if you can).

3. Take responsibility for growing your own database (because whoever owns the customer owns the gold).

Yes, it's far more work to generate your own sales and sell direct to the consumer, but at the end of the day that's where the relationship is made.

From that moment on, we took the growing of our website, DailyDeals.com.au, very seriously. We were lucky in that we could spread the risk over the four main arms of our business, but we decided to focus on this one website to see how fast we could grow it and how far we could take it.

In those early days, there were many constraints to growth, but what fuelled our passion was the fact we were all in it together. Our team was working to capacity, exhausted from the labour of the day, and working hard with minimal resources to make it all happen. This pursuit of success against the odds created a sense of camaraderie and forged firm friendships. We didn't know it at the time, but we were forming what would become the core culture of Catch.

We wish we had a photo of our magnificent team to show you, but sadly it was a different world in 2006, and we just didn't take any. ☹

(Incidentally, Vijay stayed with us for 10 years and became Chief Technology Officer (CTO) of the whole Catch group. Ferry, our first programmer, is still with Catch. He outlasted the founders!)

Nowhere to go and no way to grow

By June 2006, we had seven employees and a super mediocre website (DailyDeals.com.au) that sold about one hundred products a day. We were paying the bills, and doing okay, but no matter how hard we worked we just couldn't seem to grow the business. It felt like we were capped by our circumstances in every respect: we had limited money to buy stock, limited staff to manage the current demand, limited space to store the stock and limited manpower to source the deals. And worst of all, no quality brands wanted to sell to pure-play online sellers like us. It was incredibly frustrating and we didn't know how to fix it. We knew what we wanted to be; we just couldn't quite get there. We saw others doing it but couldn't work out how to compete.

Our early DailyDeals.com.au website, the precursor to what Catchoftheday would become*.

---

* How did we find all these old web pages? There's an amazing website called The Way Back Machine (aka www.web.archive.org). Insert any URL and you can see the archived pages. It's amazing.

The big daddy of them all was Deals Direct, Australia's first true online department store, founded by Paul Greenberg and Michael Rosenbaum, the guys who had bought the scooters from us years earlier. Deals Direct had 60 employees, a massive warehouse and was run by smart guys who knew what they were doing. They were the whale; we were the minnow. They had 5000 products; we had 100. How could we compete? We had to find a way to be different. But what was it going to be? How could we create a point of difference when we had nothing new or different to offer?

Better to copy and excel than to be original and mediocre

Woot is a US-based daily deals concept website. A friend showed it to us after a flight we were meant to catch together got delayed. (What a profitable delay that turned out to be.)

Woot's concept was simple: they sold one product every day at midnight. The deal lasted for 24 hours and then the sale was over. The website was written with a cool style of copywriting that was both arrogant and funny and had a 'I don't give a fuck' vibe to it, which we really liked.

Woot mainly sold electronic items and because the prices were so good, the items would sell out within hours—often in minutes! We liked the concept a lot. The best part? No-one in Australia had ever heard of Woot, so the concept was wide open for us to copy … er … be inspired by. Our motto had always been 'better to copy and excel than to be original and mediocre' and this was no different.

It was time to rewrite the rules.

What's in a name?

We truly believed that we could be the Woot of Australia, so we went for it. We've both never forgotten the night we chatted together on Messenger trying to come up with a name for this new-style website that would sell one product a day. The conversation went something like this:

Hezi

So, if it's one deal a day, let's call it something with 24 in the title ...

Gabby

Catch24 ...?

Hezi

Catch22 ...?

Hezi   **Gabby**

How about catch of the day?

Hezi

You gotta be mad—catch of the day?

Gabby

What are we selling, fish?

Hezi

It's too long.

And on it went. Blah, blah, blah … Anyway, after much debate, we decided on Catchoftheday.

Just to be clear, at the time of launching, none of us thought this website would be anything more than an additional stream of income to the other four we already had.

 Hezi

For the next two months, while Gabby was busy building relationships and sourcing products, Vijay, Ferry and I built the site in collaboration with a programmer we found for $1500 on oDesk who lived in some remote Ukrainian village. It was going well until we were ready to launch and the guy just suddenly disappeared! We couldn't get in touch with him for a week. I remember having sleepless nights. We had already advertised the launch date of the new website on our DailyDeals.com.au website and now our main developer was gone! I thought he'd run off with all the code and our money and was now sipping piña coladas in some bar in Kiev. Every hour during the night, I would turn on my laptop in bed to see if he had written to explain what had happened, but there was nothing. I started to lose hope. Then, one morning a few days later, I heard the sound of a message coming through on Messenger. It was him. He apologised and explained that his village got flooded; he'd lost all power for a few days and he couldn't contact us. Turns out, he was an honest man. A great developer? Not so much.

The web page we launched with was super basic: just a simple logo of a fisherman, a counter that counted down from 24 hours, a single product and a product description with a sales spiel that walked the chutzpah line of brazen, arrogant and blatant. You can see from our original web pages that we certainly didn't wait for perfection in order to launch the site.

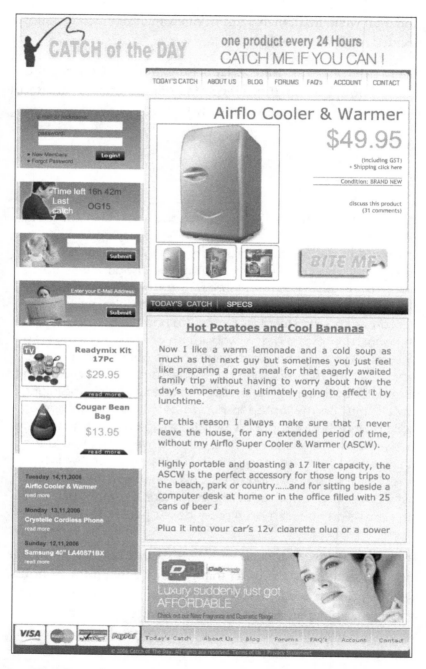

Our first iteration of the Catchoftheday website. Never forget: every first draft of anything is shit.

Here's a quick tip: don't wait for perfection to launch your website. Entrepreneurs often make the mistake of waiting for perfection before launching a product or a business, not realising that for every moment they procrastinate, they lose valuable time and money. Take our advice and just focus on the features that make the product work—that distinguish it in the market—and release it quickly to capture the opportunity. All the rest—the 'nice-to-have' features—can come later.

DON'T WAIT FOR PERFECTION TO LAUNCH YOUR WEBSITE.

As co-founder of LinkedIn Reid Hoffman said, 'If you're happy with your first draft, you've launched too late'. Or, as we like to say, the first draft of anything is shit.

Landing the first catches

Our next job was to find some amazing launch deals for our new website. We called every supplier we'd ever met, and asked them to come to the party with some sharp deals for our new site. We had no idea how hard that was going to be.

We'll never forget one of our first supplier meetings. It was with Power DC, a battery distributor run by a father-and-son team at an office just 300 metres from ours. We were so excited to tell them about our plans to launch this incredible site that would sell just one product every single day. You could tell by the look on their faces they thought we were crazy. A deal a day? On a website? Paying online with a credit card? This will never succeed! That was the response we got from most suppliers in those early days.

Our launch product was a great deal: a Thomson-branded DVD recorder for $99. We managed to source 300 of them at an amazing price, selling them for 50 per cent less than any other retailer. On the night of 18 October 2006 our team of seven was at the office at midnight awaiting the big launch countdown. The anticipation was building.

10, 9, 8, 7, 6, 5, 4, 3, 2, 1: Catchoftheday is live! Drum roll!

Within a couple of minutes we managed to sell 13 of the DVD recorders, and then *boom* ... the site crashed! We simply couldn't handle the traffic of these eager customers! For the next two hours our tech team, Vijay and Ferry, tried to solve the issues, but with no luck. The rest of us were answering emails from disappointed customers giving us crap for the miserable effort. We all got home at 4 am, had a short sleep and were back in the office by 8 am the next day. This routine continued for three days, and we were all kaput by then. This was unsustainable. Something had to change.

What did we do? We moved the launch time of our deals from midnight to midday.

Catchoftheday was born and our Fair-Etail™* was about to begin.

You're only as good as your last deal

Adding this new Catchoftheday business to our other suite of sites was not without its challenges. It put a strain on our finances, created more work for everyone and added pressure on us to find a great deal every day. And it's fair to say that without an A-grade deal each day we didn't have a business. With this newfound

---

* We made this up and like it so much, we're going to trademark it.

obligation, we began to feel the weight of customer expectations and quietly questioned why we'd started the thing at all.

We knew we could get away with 'okay' deals for a day or two—or even for three or four days—but if we had a run of seven average deals, we just knew that by day eight we were dead because customers wouldn't be coming back. On many days, at 9 am, with just hours to go before launch, we'd stare at the ceiling, praying and hoping that somehow a great deal would fall from the sky. We believed that if our customers gave us their time and trust by regularly visiting our site, our job was to make sure they were delighted and would return the next day to see what's on offer. Our livelihoods depended on it, and that's what made this business model so hard for our competitors to copy. But we pushed hard for these deals, knocked on many doors, banged on a few, and took the third door occasionally, and sure enough, the deals began to flow. Slowly, the word about our great deals began to spread.

To niche or not to niche?

After realising that we couldn't be all things to all people, and that many of our categories only had a small number of products on offer, we decided to forget about competing with Deals Direct and forge our own way by doing two things. Focusing on a narrow range of products for a specific target market and offering the products at bargain basement prices. It was a risk focusing on a narrow range of products for a specific target market at bargain basement prices. It was a risk but, in all honesty, we had no option. We couldn't afford to do it any other way.

This strategy worked because it let our customers know they were guaranteed to get the best price in the country, which made them pay attention to the deal, even if it was for something they didn't really want or need at that time. The fear of missing out on the deal made them take action.

FOMO—our secret sauce for driving sales

The best way to make a person want something is to tell them they can't have it. Even if people are not overly interested in buying something to start with, tell them they can't have it and suddenly they desperately need to have it and have it *now*.

FOMO (fear of missing out) is a powerful driver in sales and we used it to great effect. Each sale lasted for 24 hours and when the time was up, it was up, and the deal wasn't coming back again. (Well, sometimes we offered it again a few months later.)

It may seem counter-intuitive, but we loved it when items sold out within an hour or two. Some would see it as a missed opportunity, but we looked at it as good marketing. It simply meant that the following day, or the next time we sold a similar item, the order numbers would be just that much higher.

The FOMO concept can work for all sorts of businesses. For example, our favourite bakery is called Baker Bleu. They open at 7.30 am every day and by 8 am there's a massive queue of customers waiting for their dose of … bread. Yes, people actually wait for 40 minutes to get bread. And guess what? There's none left by 1 pm. No bread for you! Yes, they can make more, but why would they? That 'Sold Out' sign is the best generator of word-of-mouth recommendation you can get.

Using FOMO is a common tactic in marketing now. Trivago, Booking.com and most airlines (the ones still in business) all use the FOMO principle on their website booking forms. Phrases like '10 people looking at this now', '3 seats left at this price' and '5 people booked this room in the last 10 minutes' are all clever ways of getting you to part with your hard-earned money.

P.S. FOMO won't work if the quality of the product is poor. Baker Bleu's bread is amazing, which is why people keep coming back. Likewise, our Catchoftheday deals were amazing too, which is why our customers kept coming back. If your quality is poor, the customers won't return, the queues will dry up and your business will fail.

The strategy also made our product the very best deal available on any given day, saving us a huge amount of time and money by not having to stock thousands of products. Instead, we were able to purchase thousands of a single product at an incredible price, which resulted in us getting a better deal. We also sold more of it than any other website selling the same item.

While this focus allowed us to dramatically improve our profits, it did have a drawback. We knew we couldn't please everyone and that some people would get upset with us if the deal of the day was not to their liking. But we also knew that there were enough boring department stores out there selling the same stuff already, and that if people wanted to buy the traditional way in a traditional store, there were plenty of places they could do so. We just weren't going to be one of them.

Through trial and error (and a bit of luck—more on that in a moment!) we had stumbled on a formula that was exponentially more economical and better suited to our limited resources, and it was working.

There's luck, and there's *Mazal*

You don't get lucky sitting on the sofa with your arms crossed. You get lucky by being out there in the world, making things happen. So, what exactly is luck? Sweat, effort, chance, intuition? It's all that and more, but the best definition we know comes from the Hebrew term *Mazal* (MZL)*: location, timing and learning.

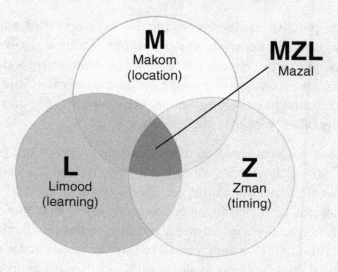

When all three intersect, great things happen:

- *M (Makom): location*. You need to position yourself in the right location to take advantage of opportunities that present themselves. Go to events, conferences and trade shows, and ask for meetings with people who can help you reach your dreams.

- *Z (Zman): time*. Timing is (almost) everything. There are so many examples of great business ideas that simply got their timing all wrong or were just too early, or too late.

---

*Thank you to Lior Shoham for introducing us to this concept.

- *L (Limood): learning.* You need to keep learning all the time. Learning equips us to solve problems, to identify issues, to have the confidence to question the status quo and to think of different ways to solve problems. Without learning new ways, how do you expect to improve or cause change? We have been reading industry news from sites such as TechCrunch and Bloomberg for years.

CHAPTER 3
Gaining momentum

By early 2007 we still had only seven staff, but our revenue and the volume of transactions were growing rapidly. From a rocky start of selling just $1000 worth of goods a day, we were now selling $10 000 a day worth across all three sites: eBay, DailyDeals. com.au and Catchoftheday. These figures were never going to put the big retailers out of business, but we were energetic, motivated and excited to see our figures grow. We had no inkling we were creating a billion-dollar business! We were just like a bunch of kids having fun playing with computers.

From the get-go, it was very clear that there were three parties needed to make this business work: Catch-supplier-customer. Without customers, we had no business. Without suppliers, we had no deals to attract customers.

From our early days of buying, we realised that all suppliers—no matter how good they are—make mistakes when buying. There is a joke in the retail world: 'The buyer is always wrong'. They either buy too much, or too little. Being the buyers at Catchoftheday, we understood the meaning behind this joke and lived it every single day—and any buyer reading this book right now is surely nodding their head in agreement.

WE REALISED THAT THERE WAS A

MASSIVE UNTAPPED OPPORTUNITY

IN BEING ABLE TO HELP SUPPLIERS AND BRANDS GET RID OF THEIR 'MISTAKES', AND THIS WAS THE PIECE OF THE PUZZLE THAT CATCHOFTHEDAY SOLVED.

We are better buyers!

Suppliers get caught out with excess stock for lots of reasons. It could be that a big retailer cancels an order; the wrong colours or sizes are ordered; the wrong items are sent out; the boxes get damaged; or the buyer overestimates consumer demand, such as having too many air conditioners in the middle of winter. What we were looking for were deals where the suppliers were willing to let go of stock at stupidly low prices in order to free up warehouse space or to receive much-needed cash to pay for the next container of goods. We realised that there was a massive untapped opportunity in being able to help suppliers and brands get rid of their 'mistakes', and this was the piece of the puzzle that Catchoftheday solved.

One of the questions we get asked all the time is, 'Why has Catchoftheday succeeded in e-commerce while others have not?' and while there are many ways to answer this question, our answer has always been, quite simply, 'We are better buyers!'

 Gabby

In our first three years of business, I was the primary buyer for most of our products. As I look back, these were *the* best years of my life.

The challenge of building something from nothing and seeing it grow and succeed is a feeling that can't be replicated.

Our Catch buyers working in the business today don't know how lucky they are because, today, Catch is a brand that everyone wants to be associated with and work with. That was not always the case. 'No!' was the supplier's default answer, and we had to work super hard to get them to hear us out. Now, all our buyers receive the red-carpet treatment. Suppliers love our buyers because they know they can help them shift stock others can't.

I really enjoyed those early days of buying and door kicking, and I continued doing so until 2012. Later on, I realised that there are better buyers than me and it was time to pass the baton to the next generation: Anees, Guy, Kalman and Adam, I'm talking about you!

Being a great buyer is a skill that can't be taught at university, and it can't be inherited either. You either have it or you don't.

We called our buyers 'product hunters', because they hunted down great deals and brought them to the door of our customers.

While you've either got the talent or you ain't, here are a few strategies anyone can develop that will make you a better buyer.

- *Be curious:* read sales catalogues, or just walk through shopping centres and have a look around. Curiosity goes hand in hand with learning; the more you immerse yourself in your niche, the more educated you will become. Knowing your category allows you to spot a deal the moment it comes your way. Great entrepreneurial companies and individuals always ask 'why?', and that curiosity powers their creativity.

- *Be an honest person, and do the right thing:* this is the quickest way to build trust. If you're a jerk, the word will quickly get around. We always believed that honesty (and integrity) are the best policies.

- *Build a relationship with your seller:* everyone prefers to deal with a friend rather than just a faceless executive hiding behind an email.

- *Pay your suppliers on time:* even better, pay them ahead of time. They'll never forget you.

Guy Polak, Catch's head of buying, knows exactly how to build relationships.

Guy

We always treat the suppliers that we source our goods from as friends. We figured out quickly that in order for a business transaction to take place, both parties have to benefit; it has to be a win-win relationship. It just has to. A relationship can only continue and thrive if both parties are happy over the long term. Some people will try and screw their suppliers over. We never do that. For us, it is never about making a great profit on deal number one; it is always about making the supplier happy so they choose to come back to us for deals two, three and 100.

Never forget that people do business with people they like. So how do you become likeable? Again, this is a tough question because you either have that quality or you don't, but generally speaking, good buyers need to be outgoing, talkative types who can win a room over and build rapport. If you aren't good at that, get good at it or find another person to do the buying.

Second, you don't create business by telling people, 'I want to do business with you'. You create business by building relationships, and you do that by connecting and finding common ground between you and the other person. For example, once you figure out what someone is interested in, throw some random but related knowledge into the conversation. You don't need to be an expert on every topic; just think of something to take the conversation from awkward to exciting. Once you have the other person feeling comfortable, you can start to build that bridge.

 ## Gabby

I often use sport, and in particular soccer, as a bridge to build relationships. I live and breathe the game and can always steer the conversation to a team, location, match or player that is relevant to my customer. It's such a global game so I always find something that is personal to them. For example, if I meet someone from Hungary, I will throw in the name of Ferenc Puskás, the best Hungarian player ever; and if someone is from Brazil, I will steer the conversation towards my visit during the World Cup. This always makes people smile and puts them at ease. You can steer the conversation to any topic that's relevant to the situation—it might be music, what you're watching on Netflix, or if you're desperate, or from Melbourne, the weather.

People do business with people they like, and being likeable is as simple as showing an interest in what the other person feels passionate about. In business the financial benefit is obvious, but at the end of the day we all want to surround ourselves with nice people, both in our social life and especially in our business life.

 ## Hezi

When building a new relationship, I actually like to put a lot of effort into researching the other person's business and finding out what their responsibilities are within that business. Then I ask lots of questions to fill the gaps in order to understand their personal and professional challenges, opportunities and goals. This puts me in a better position to find a way to help us exchange value in a fair deal for all.

Adam Chrapot, Catch's head of sourcing, has a PhD in relationship building.

Adam

I have always firmly believed in the theory that you catch more flies with honey than vinegar. Wherever possible I always build a meaningful and personal relationship with our suppliers as, quite simply, you get more business this way. When suppliers are your friends, they feel comfortable dealing with you, they know they can trust you and they are more likely to satisfy your particular requirements. Most importantly, you become top of mind and will be the first customer they call when they have a great deal. This proved to be incredibly valuable and successful when building the Catch supply chain.

Here are five more tips that will help you build better relationships.

1. *Meet in person*. You can't fall in love unless you go on a date, which is why relationships are best built face to face. It is far too easy to misconstrue feelings over email or even a phone call, so make the effort to meet over a coffee, even for a five-minute chat or an afternoon walk at the beach. You'll quickly see the relationship move to the next level. Our suppliers knew this and worked hard to get in front of us. We often got invited by a supplier to events like a music concert, the Grand Prix or the Australian Open tennis. Why? Because our suppliers knew it was by far the best (and cheapest) way to build a meaningful relationship with us. Once you build a personal relationship, everyone feels a lot more comfortable doing business because now you're friends rather than just distant business associates.

2. *Don't leave voicemails*. No-one listens to them anymore. If you don't get the person, hang up and ring back.

3. *Be funny*. Like it or not, 'funny is money' and people will always prefer doing business with someone who makes them laugh. Why? Because life is meant to be fun and those who can combine business and fun will get the sale over those who can't take, or make, a joke. Don't be too serious! This approach has certainly worked for us.

4. *Don't get angry over email*. We have Mediterranean tempers so when we get upset it is very tempting to respond in an aggressive or angry way. Our tip? Count to 100 and then

respond. You will almost always be thankful you didn't act in haste.

5.   *Never, ever close a door.* Doors are very hard to open so it's your job to keep them open. Some suppliers might piss you off today, but they can be your best friend tomorrow, or even a year or two down the track. Besides, if they leave their current job, you want to make sure they say nice things about you at their next job.

So, we knew the art of buying, and we knew suppliers had a massive problem that we could fix. Now we just needed to convince them we were the ones to fix it for them. Here's the spiel we used when we'd turn up in our van trying to convince a supplier to sell to us.

Hi Joe,

I'm from Catchoftheday. We are an online shopping site. Our specialty is purchasing end-of-line stock and clearance offers. We buy the goods on the spot. I will make an immediate decision. I will pay you for the goods today and I will take the goods with me now. Is there anything in the warehouse you need to clear?

Here's what Joe really heard:

I will pay you today and take the goods now.

How could Joe say no to an offer like that?

Innovate or die

At some point, all suppliers and retailers get caught out with too much stock. We did too. So, we came up with a solution to get rid of it. We called it the Catchathon, a 'monthly megasale' of all the stuff we got stuck with at the warehouse. The sale took place on the last Thursday of every month.

While most of our deals were simply unbelievable, we couldn't expect all our customers to show up every day to buy from us, so the reality was, they missed out on some of these great deals. The Catchathon gave them an opportunity to 'catch up' on a product they may have missed.

The first Catchathon had 33 products, but as the popularity grew, so did the numbers. Within a couple of years, our Catchathons had as many as 1000 products, and we stretched the event over two days, generating gross profit of $500 000 over that two-day period (yes, that's gross profit!).

From that day on, we ran it every single month, and, almost without exception, it has been the bestselling day of the month. We discovered two very important lessons from this innovation: that selling 33 of our best products on a single day generates more profits than selling one product; and it's okay to break the rules (of selling one deal a day), especially if you're the one making the rules.

Say 'thank you'

We've had thousands of suppliers help us on our journey. We can't mention them all, but we are thankful to all of them. Here is a story about one of them that deserves special credit.

JTC was a small import/export business run by two brilliant buyers called Carl and Tom. We met them when we drove by their warehouse, 400 metres away from our Moorabbin office. Like Catch, they sourced end-of-line and clearance deals in very large volumes, and then sold their wares to retailers such as the $2 Shop.

For bargain hunters like us, walking into JTC was like being a kid in Disneyland. We'd visit them three to four times a week, checking out the latest stock arrivals and seeing if we could find any tasty catches for our customers.

Carl was used to selling six of this or 12 of that at any one time to his mum-and-dad retailers so when he saw us coming, he could see a massive opportunity to accelerate his business. He helped us figure out what we could and could not sell, and even volunteered to put together boxes of themed products, like Dora the Explorer or Thomas the Tank Engine, that we could sell for $10 so we didn't have to 'pick and pack' the boxes ourselves. This helped us create A-grade deals, gave the customer a 'surprise and delight' moment and helped us overcome the immense pressure of having to conjure up a daily deal from nowhere.

After one year in business, we closed off 2007 with sales of $7.69 million, with more than $1 million of that sourced from JTC. It's numbers like these that propelled us to 45th place on the BRW Fast 100 List—and it made our day. Being featured in *BRW* (*Business Review Weekly*) was super cool and a 'first' we will remember forever. (Other notable starters on the list that year were local start-ups Atlassian, with revenues of $22 million, and Aconex, with revenues of $28 million. They've both done all right since then.)

Without the help provided by people such as Tom and Carl, none of this would have been possible, so remember to say 'thanks' to those who helped you along the way.

A Catchathon event. Our best selling day of the month.

Necessity is the mother of invention

Finding an A-grade deal every day looked simple, but every daily deal had to meet our high standards, which made the process complicated. The deal had to:

- 'surprise and delight' our customers
- appeal to a wide range of people
- sell in large numbers
- be super profitable so we could pay the bills of this fast-growing business.

Sure, it was a challenge to achieve all this in one deal, but it forced us to get more creative in finding new and different ways to sell in those kinds of volumes.

For example, some of the merchandising innovations we came up with to shift old stock included classy creations such as The Box of Crap (affectionately known as the Box of Pooki). This was a bag or box containing a bunch of random items from our warehouse that we needed to clear. The message to customers? You get what you get and you don't get upset.

Here are some other event ideas we came up with:

- the $10 Day: where all items are $10 or less
- the $28 Day: all products sell for $28 including shipping (not one of our best ones, it only lasted for three months)
- the Mega Baby Box: 10 items for your baby for $30 (we sold thousands!)
- the Jewellery Megabox: 25 pieces of jewellery, normally valued at $400; we sold them for $25 (people often ask us how we sold packages of expensive jewellery for so little. See lesson for our secret to this one.)

- the School Essential Megabox: 15 items for kids going back to school (this did well during COVID-19!)

- the Box of Real Crap: it was as the name suggests (and it was our top-selling box; our customers loved this one the best of all!).

Turning trash into treasure

Four hundred dollars' worth of jewellery for $25. Ten quality baby products for $30. Free products! Just pay for shipping!

How did we make all these amazing deals happen? How did we turn what others would consider trash, into treasure? To fully understand how we did it, you need to know we considered ourselves to be 'solution providers' to our suppliers. They had a problem. We had the solution and we found innovative ways that enabled everyone to win.

For example, here's the background on how we 'created' the $400 jewellery box for $25.

You know all those teenage fashion stores at your local mall? They have rows and rows of trendy necklaces, rings, bangles, hair accessories and the like. Fashion and trends change quickly, and so does jewellery, so twice a year the retailer had to get rid of vast amounts of unsold items. Generally, someone in the retail store would go through the stands and tip hundreds of random jewellery items into dozens of large boxes, in no order or tidy fashion, seal the boxes up and send them to us. We'd open the boxes, tip the contents onto the floor of the warehouse, sift through *all* the items and sort them into homogenous groups so we could see what we had. It was a mess! Or as we call it in Hebrew, *balagan!*

It's important to note that all these items were in tip top condition, had barcodes and labels still attached, and often the price tag as well. The brands were first class. We can't divulge the prices of these items, of course, but most retailed for an average of $20.

Our next step was to 'curate' each and every box of jewellery to make sure that every lady who received it would, upon opening the box, scream 'Hallelujah!'. That was our goal, and we achieved it. The feedback was phenomenal: 'Can't believe how you do it!', 'Amazing value!', 'Thank you!' and so on. This curation and picking and packing process required a lot of hard work, but let's just say that we bought the goods at such a low price that it was worth the effort. The triple win. The suppliers were happy, the customers were happy, and Catchoftheday was happy too.

These marketing campaigns worked like crazy. Sales kept growing and records were broken every single day. It was a thrilling time and without a doubt one of the most innovative years in our history.

Our single biggest challenge in building Catch was getting suppliers to sell to us. As far as most retailers were concerned back then, the party was at Bricks and Mortar. As such, we often encountered measured resistance from local suppliers and brands. They just would not sell to us. They were traditional, stuck in their ways and unable to see what the future held.

So, when we came along and upset the applecart, they didn't like it very much and scrambled to find reasons not to do business with us. The most common excuse they gave was,

'Sorry, we don't sell to companies without a physical storefront'.

Can you believe that? It sounds laughable now, but that's what they said.

Catch was already 18 months old by this stage, shifting millions of dollars' worth of stock every month, and yet nine out of 10 reputable suppliers and brands still refused to sell goods to us because we didn't have a front door.

As we write this book, COVID-19 is in full swing and everyone is in lockdown. All the shopping centres are closed, but, interestingly, Catch and all the other e-commerce players are still well and truly open for business, busier than ever and able to support their customers and suppliers during this difficult patch. How things change!

Looking back, it's hard to imagine that no-one wanted to sell goods to us because we didn't have a physical shop.

Our big break

One of the toughest segments for us to crack was the PC and computer accessories market. Prior to March 2008, we had not been able to source a single deal from this segment. It was a closed shop, with the retailers and suppliers all cosy in bed together and very happy with their lot, thank you very much.

When we did crack it, however, all of that changed in a major way. Looking back, this was the turning point in our trajectory that catapulted us into the league of uber-retailers. Here's how we cracked it.

Gabby

The computer and tech segments were controlled by a small number of massive distributors. The largest one in Australia was a company called Ingram Micro. By pure chance I heard that they were hosting an invite-only evening conference for their clients. I didn't get an invitation; nor did anyone I knew. It was a well-guarded industry. But that didn't stop me. I ironed my suit (not something I wear often, except at weddings) and fronted up to the Melbourne Exhibition Centre. I honestly can't remember how I did it, but I somehow kicked my way in with an exuberant display of charm, ignorance and chutzpah!

I came armed with 100 A4 flyers that detailed the message of Catchoftheday—and I'm glad I brought them. There were around eighty suppliers, all lined up in rows, each displaying their wares. Each stand was manned by the local distributor ready to do business. I went to work. I had only one evening, 80 potential new suppliers and one chance to make a first impression. I moved from stand to stand, shaking hands, handing out flyers and telling everyone how great Catchoftheday could be for their business.

That night I sowed the seeds for ongoing relationships that shaped the years to come and would prove fruitful beyond belief. Some of the blue-chip companies I connected with that night include Toshiba, Asus, Canon, HP, Lexmark, Compaq, Polaroid, SanDisk and Verbatim, just to name a few.

The following week, we were bombarded with offers from all of those companies wanting us to feature their products: laptops, printers, hard drives, cameras, storage devices, memory cards and more laptops. Suddenly, we had the premium brands all the retailers had. This paved the way for other big brands to do business with us as they soon realised they too could sell their premium brands to us—and make a lot of money doing so.

Anees, our 21-year-old junior copywriter, took the calls. Until his arrival a year earlier, we had done the copywriting, and, to be honest,

We are Daily Deals. A company featuring a number of highly successful sales channels with the ability to move astonishing amounts of stock. Our various initiatives include one of Australia's largest TV shopping campaigns with regular infomercials on all morning shows, be it Kerry Anne or Channel 7.

Furthermore we also run one of the Australia's top online department stores **www.dailydeals.com.au** and the latest shopping addiction to sweep the nation, everyone's favourite, **www.catchoftheday.com.au**. While **Daily Deals** offers us the perfect platform to move a wide variety of stock around the clock, with its fresh and unique **'New Day, New Deal'** concept the **Catch of the Day** is one of the hottest websites to hit our country.

In our short history we have earned wide acclaim and numerous awards, the most recent of which is placement in the **BRW Fastest Growing 100**. For those of you not in the loop, Business Review Weekly, one of Australia's premier financial periodicals publishes an annual list of Australia's fastest growing companies.

We operate from a large 4000m² complex featuring our massive retail outlet (see photos) and a state of the art dispatch centre.

With access to multiple channels we are well positioned to deal with closeout deals and surplus orders.

Daily Deals
2215 Princes Hwy
Mulgrave, Victoria 3170
Australia

Gabby Leibovich
Mobile:
Email: gabby@dailydeals.com.au
Ph: +61 3 9558 5640, Fax: +61 3 9558 5736

Gabby: Here's the flyer I took to the life-changing Ingram Micro event. This event was the turning point for Catch, and this flyer helped us break through.

we were not that great at it, but someone had to do it. It wasn't long before he became an integral part of our growing team of 15 staff and our right-hand man. Prior to joining us, Anees had never sold a thing in his life, but he was a fast learner and could turn his hand to anything. He taught himself graphic design, handled the sales calendar of deals, and started to accompany us to meetings with suppliers. At this stage he was lacking the confidence to be the main man, but all that would change within a couple of years. In the following months, with his help, we experienced the fastest and strongest growth to date. Here are just some of the fabulous sales results we achieved back in 2008:

- 4000 Asus computers in less than 38 minutes!

- 800+ units of external hard drives in a single day

- 10 000 power boards (we made a profit of $100 000 that day!)

- 320 000 Ferrero Rocher chocolate balls in seven hours

- 11 000 coin counters in one day.

 Hezi

I've always tried to challenge a new recruit when they join the company.

My main objective was for them to quickly adopt the philosophy of 'just because it's always been done like that, doesn't mean it's the best way to do it'.

When Anees joined, he very quickly became quite good at buying and selling, both fairly new skills for him. He became quite a master over the years. So, after a few months when he was getting quite confident and thought he had now learned it all, I noticed that while he was a super negotiator at getting the lowest price, he still lacked the skill to price things correctly. One example I remember was an electronic device that regularly sold in other stores for $100 and the wholesale price was $80. By some miracle, we managed to buy 1000 units from a supplier at wholesale for $20. It was an unbelievable price. Anees put them on the website for $29, in line with our normal margins but without taking advantage of our unusually low wholesale price. Why? Simply because that's how a lot of our buyers were doing it. The 1000 units sold out in two hours and it was a great day.

Lighting struck twice and by another miracle, a few months later the supplier had another 1000 units and we took the lot. Anees was about to put them back on the site for $29 and I challenged him to price them at $69.99. He thought I was mad, saying 'that's almost triple the price we sold them for last time!' He was really starting to sweat. I told him, 'You've based your original price not on market demand but rather on a habit. You've based it on a formula that you've seen people in our business use over and over, but you must treat every opportunity on its own unique factors.'

He gave it a shot and listed them at $69.99. We still sold all 1000 units for quadruple the profit in the same amount of time. Anees was a fast learner. In fact, he learned so fast and was so good that it was he who came along with us to meet an investor when it was time to set a valuation for our entire business.

Sale of the century

When we arrived in Australia in late 1986 (Gabby was at year 11, Hezi was at grade 4), our favourite TV show was *Sale of the Century*. Every night at 7 our whole family would sit down and watch Tony Barber do his thing. Not only did we get to play a trivia game, but we also improved our English. Our most memorable 'sale of the century' was the Toshiba laptop.

In July 2008, Toshiba offered to sell us 8000 laptops, which we were able to sell for $599 per unit. Generally, we liked committing to and paying for goods at the time of purchase because it always allowed us to negotiate hard and get a great deal.

On this occasion, however, we simply didn't have $4 000 000 in cash lying around to pay for the stock. But one of the great advantages of running a 24-hour-deal business is that the sales cycle is also 24 hours, or less. We seriously wanted to do this deal so we advised Toshiba that we would run the deal on Wednesday of that week, and would advise them of our sales quantity the following day. Toshiba had nothing to lose.

The deal went nuts. It started at midday and by 4 pm we had sold 4000 laptops.

That's 1000 laptops per hour!

The whole office was buzzing with excitement. But the deal was short lived. Rumour has it that not long after the deal started, Toshiba received an urgent call from a very large PC retailer (we can't reveal the name) and as a result of that call, we were notified we had to stop the sale at 4 pm and leave the remaining 4000 laptops unsold. That's hardly normal behaviour—but it is what it is.

The news of the deal spread like wildfire. Within hours, *every* supplier and retailer of PCs in the country had heard about this crazy Melbourne website that was offering unbelievable products (and eating into their margins). This was the day our reputation was made. We had made the big league. We can't think of a single local retailer that could purchase 4000 laptops of one model, move them in a day and pay for the goods before dispatch. Not today, and certainly not back in 2008.

Catching fire

The word about Catchoftheday was spreading fast. That one deal sealed our reputation, and from there the new deals flowed like water. One day we sold 2000 Asus laptops in a single hour; the

This Toshiba laptop deal put us on the map and opened the door for deals to flow freely. It was a game changer for us.

next day we shifted 10 000 pillow sets in five hours; the following day we sold 8000 pearl necklaces. The deals just kept coming and so did lots of new customers, each discovering us for the first time. We continued to create crazy promotions that kept our customers hungry and excited for more. We found out first hand that nothing could beat a word-of-mouth recommendation from a friend or a workmate. Everyone loved our bargains, and everyone loved showing off their latest toy, shoe or electronic gadget. The addiction was growing.

Our trusty office whiteboard, which contained the matrix that mapped and tracked all our deals, was filling fast with silly events such as the Scentathon (perfumes galore), Mamathon (deals for mum), Papathon (obvious) and Freeday (where everything is free and the customer just pays for shipping). Would you believe that on our first 'free day' we made a clear profit of $200 000 in a single day selling items for free!

WE MADE A CLEAR PROFIT OF $200 000 IN A SINGLE DAY SELLING ITEMS FOR FREE!

These and many others deals like this kept the excitement level on a high, day after day. The need to innovate and stay ahead of the curve forced us to be working at the edge all the time. It was exhilarating for everyone. Even today, Catch still features these events, and many of the concepts have been copied and used by retailers all over the world. We were creating a whole new way to retail, and we didn't even know it.

By this stage, the new kid on the block was running faster than anyone could have imagined. So much so, we shut down our eBay operation, switched off the As Seen on TV channel and closed the DailyDeals.com.au site to focus our efforts exclusively on Catchoftheday. We hired some talented team members to help us keep up, including Carlo, our photographer and designer;

Pooven, Vijay's brother, who worked in operations; and Kalman Polak, who joined us as our store manager. You'll read more about them later.

In August 2008 we relocated to a building in Springvale, 29 kilometres south-east of Melbourne. We were expanding big time in every way. The building was composed of a much larger warehouse of 2000 m², a small office of 200 m² and a retail store of 2000 m². Retail store? Yes, we did open our doors to the public. We were hoping that having a physical street presence would satisfy the many suppliers that were still unwilling to supply online-only retailers like us. We were also looking to win a few extra customers and make them aware of our online offering. We found this to be a great customer acquisition channel for our maturing website.

The retail store was short lived. On 23 December 2008, just six months after opening, in the busiest week of the year, on the busiest day of that week, our store and warehouse was flooded by a massive downpour of torrential rain. The entire office was knee deep in water. Every employee worked back and spent the whole night in the warehouse moving all the stock that was sitting on the floor to higher ground. Eventually, we managed to locate a company to bring in some water-sucking equipment to help extract the water from the warehouse. The fact it took 20 hours to remove it all tells you just how much water there was. That storm was a turning point for the store. We never reopened and we unfortunately missed out on the Boxing Day sales season, the biggest retail month of the year. It took us 10 years to give bricks and mortar another try, (but there's a lot of reading to go until you get to that bit …)

One last thing …

We can't not mention this one deal. If the Toshiba deal put us on the map, this Samsung one redefined the boundaries. In January

2009, between the hours of 12 noon and 1 pm, we sold $1 500 000 worth of Samsung TVs. Yes, you read that correctly: $1.5 million in *one hour*. If we could go back in time and recreate one moment from our history, this would be it: that moment our small team gathered around the computer, staring at the screen in disbelief, watching these phenomenal numbers roll in. We truly felt we were in some kind of parallel world, but we weren't. This was real, this was Catchoftheday and we were here to stay.

Anees and Carlo, two of our early hires and loyal team members from the old days. Working hard, as usual! (Behind them you can see VJ—yes, another Vijay! He worked on that machine for 10 years and was one of the best warehouse team members we had. He is still at Catch!)

CHAPTER 4

Recession? Shmecession!

In 2009, the clouds of recession were brewing on the horizon. The US stock market had crashed and as they used to say, 'When the US coughs, the rest of the world catches a cold'. It's well known that when a recession hits, consumers close their wallets, especially on retail and luxury items. For us at Catchoftheday, nothing could have been further from the truth.

By now we were well established as a clearance house and this recession created incredible opportunities for businesses like ours. Suppliers stuck with stock came knocking like never before.

Cancelled orders, slow-moving items, customers not buying—the supplier's pain was our gain. The recession was a perfect storm that Catchoftheday needed.

While a recession can hurt many people, we were fortunate in that we were able to play Robin Hood in some ways by giving consumers access to deals the big retailers just couldn't offer. These deals genuinely helped households hit hard by the recession to save money and reduce the impact the recession had on so many.

As we write these words, the world is in the midst of the COVID-19 pandemic, and we're fighting each other for the last roll of toilet paper at the supermarkets. The future right now is worryingly unclear, but what is clear is that many businesses will not survive this storm because only the strongest businesses can thrive during tough times. Catchoftheday is one of them. We have truly built a recession-proof, COVID-19-proof, bullet-proof business that will be here for many years to come.

That recession of 2009 brought us many opportunities, such as the attention of *Today Tonight*. We'd been wanting to be featured on national TV for a long time and now was our chance. We can split our Catch experience into two eras: before our appearance on *Today Tonight*, and after our appearance on *Today Tonight*. The difference was like … well … day and night. Watch the video on our website, catchofthedecade.com.au.

How four minutes of fame made us a fortune

We knew TV was powerful; we just didn't know how powerful. After a big day at the Catch office selling millions of dollars' worth of goods, Gabby went on air and in four minutes created a segment that would reap huge rewards for us the following day. His TV script went something like this:

In just 24 hours, we sold $1.4 million worth of goods. 550 TVs. 80 vacuum cleaners. 600 handbags. Recession? Shmecession! Thousands of parcels leave this building every single day … We are one of Australia's top three department stores … We are Australia Post's biggest client …

… and on it went.

The results were phenomenal. Within 24 hours of the show airing, more than 50 000 new members joined the database. It had previously taken us 12 months to sign up 50 000 new members. In other words, we achieved in one night what had previously taken us a year.

Watching our first segment air and then seeing the sales results the next day reaffirmed our commitment to getting as much media coverage as we could. We estimated each appearance on TV was worth an extra $100 000 in sales.

Who said PR doesn't work?

We are the Amazon of Australia.

We are Australia's most watched shopping site.

We are Australia's number-one e-commerce group.

It's lines like these that got us noticed by the media. We were a tiny ship on the retail ocean so we had to do something special to get attention. Even with the best business idea in the world, if no-one knows about you, you've got nothing.

PR was our primary way of getting noticed as it built credibility. This gave the consumer confidence. Confidence built trust. Without trust, people won't buy from you, and so the cycle continues. So, how do you get people to pay attention? Get some good PR. Here are a few tips.

- *Be relevant and targeted:* do your research and tailor your media pitch accordingly. For example, business or finance journalists will want statistics and facts to support your claims of growth or leadership. If you are pitching to TV, provide them with colourful images that make the story sizzle. For one Christmas TV feature, 40 members of our warehouse team dressed up in Santa outfits, with Gabby as head Santa leading the troops!

Christmas was peak season for us so we courted the media like crazy, and it's images like this—colourful and fun—that really got us coverage. Each four-minute segment was worth at least $100 000 in sales to us.

- *Build relationships:* we always strived to be helpful and of value to the media by providing them with trend data and insights to help them build their stories. We also gave them exclusive news opportunities and were available when they needed a comment. All the business journalists had our mobile numbers and knew they could call us at any time. We quite often got called by TV channels asking to do a story within an hour or two. When that happened, we dropped everything and rushed to the chosen location.

- *Be brave:* to become a memorable brand you need to stand for something and defend that territory. Catch is synonymous with great prices. We never shied away from having an opinion, especially when we saw our customers being ripped off by the major retailers, and we actively supported our position with stories and data that brought this message to life.

- *Be excited:* if you're not excited about your story/business/ message, why should the journalist be?

Gabby: When the media called, we jumped into action. Often I had shorts and thongs on. Just as well they only shot from the waist up!

- *Build the story for the reporter:* journalists are time poor and often may decline a story because they don't have the time to cover it. Make it easy for them to say 'yes' by bringing to them what they need to easily build the story. People often asked how we got so many TV stories that were pretty much like ads. We invested a lot of time in building out the media assets so we could give them a fully packaged story. These packages contained comparison pricing data, crazy deals, details of customers willing to be filmed in their home and full access to our warehouse. We even got Australia Post involved as part of the story. We put the work in and it paid off.

- *Tell stories with data:* if you want to be an authority in your space, then being able to talk to trends and provide predictions is a great way to build that position, as well as provide media with a new and interesting perspective. Catch is a data-driven company, so we were able to build insightful stories that revealed how people shopped and what they bought, and provided predictions around future shopping trends.

- *Preparation is key:* every interview is an opportunity to tell your story, and in order to do that you need to pre-plan the key points you want to get across. Build out a number of key messages for different scenarios in readiness for guiding any interview opportunity as it arises. If you're going on TV, wear a branded T-shirt so people are visually reminded of who you represent.

 ## Gabby

I remember my first ever TV appearance. I was shitting myself and had butterflies fluttering in my tummy, but I was fully rehearsed. I knew what I was going to say as I had practised it a hundred times and I was ready to rock. The key is to be like an actor and deliver your message in a natural, spontaneous and fun way even though you've planned it.

- *Be consistent:* successful PR is a marriage, not a one-off date. To see success, you need to maintain a presence in the media and be consistent so you can maintain your share of voice and be recognised by the media as the 'go-to' expert for that story. PR has been the core element of our marketing communications and has been critical to positioning us as a trusted household brand.

We had always been pretty good at going out and getting our own PR, but the professionals do it the best. Here's Melissa Shawyer from The PR Group on how and why we as a team were able to generate millions of dollars in coverage.

Melissa

I still remember when we first connected with Catch. It was a Friday night. I was on Twitter scouring for opportunities. I came across a call-out from someone asking for recommendations of 'great tech PR agencies'. I replied, 'I run a great tech PR agency' and after a quick chat, set up a call for the next day.

When I spoke with Gabby the following day, he had just returned from holiday and was in the warehouse. A quick call turned into a two-hour discussion and by Monday I was appointed. These guys worked fast!

Walking into Catch's offices, what immediately struck me was the energy. Everyone embraced the same level of excitement and passion as the founders. I entered the boardroom expecting just Gabby and Hezi, but it was filled with a dozen people, from the department heads and buyers to the team leaders and junior staff who worked on the frontline. Everyone was on deck.

Later that day Gabby texted me and said, 'Glad you wore jeans. If you'd come in a suit we wouldn't have hired you. It's not our culture.' That clear understanding of the Catch culture has fuelled their success in business and in PR. They knew what they stood for: authenticity, fun and dynamism.

The brothers were PR naturals and knew exactly how to make PR work for them. Gabby was a master at knowing what customers wanted and how to create a shopping event that would drive talk-ability. Our strategy was to use the power of mass media to create awareness and drive traffic to the site and social media to further fuel the buzz. 'Social media is word of mouth on steroids,' he would often say. He was right.

In the early years Catch dominated TV. We wanted all Australians to know that Catch was synonymous with having the biggest product range and offering incredible value, and what better way to communicate that than through Catch's crazy shopping events? From $1 shopping days; to massive birthday events where the customers got the presents; to calling out the massive mark-ups that the fragrance and cosmetic retailers made. As a team, we spent a lot of time curating the deals, sourcing pricing comparisons and staging the story so the production crew could get an entertaining segment.

The key to their success was they saw the value PR delivered to the brand and prioritised media opportunities. Gabby was always available to workshop ideas and got involved in making these a success. From dressing up in a Halloween outfit, to riding a Razor scooter on set, to being placed in a roll cage and elevated high in the warehouse, to repeatedly sliding down the incredibly steep slide that connected level one and ground floor at their offices, just so a photographer could get the perfect picture.

Few clients I've worked with were as dedicated to getting PR as the Catch team. And it showed up in their results.

Start by taking small risks

To take big risks you need to start by taking little risks. Sometimes that means spending money to make money. When the business was just 18 months old, we had a close-knit team of around 10 guys. One of them was Carlo, our graphic designer and photographer. At that time, we were running $10 deal days and offering 30 products per day, and while Carlo was a fast worker, he could only go so quickly, which meant we were capped at offering 30 products because that's all he could cope with in a day.

This created a bit of a bottleneck in the workflow and prevented us from selling as much as we could. We debated for six months as to whether we could afford to get Carlo an assistant designer. It was a big decision as this extra salary would cost us $50 000 a year, which was a lot for us.

After much debate, we hired Lyly, our first ever female staff member, to become Carlo's deputy. It was a great decision. In the first month after her arrival, we were able to increase our graphic design output and instead of offering 30 products per day, were able to offer 100 products per day. The increase in revenue paid for Lyly's salary in no time.

Taking risks is a trait that becomes easier with repetition. Once you have taken a small risk and succeeded, you will be tempted to take bigger risks as your business progresses. Catch now has more than 500 staff members, and more than half of those are female, so here's to Lyly and to taking small risks!

How to stay ahead

People often ask us, 'How did you keep ahead of the rest?' and 'How did you know what the next big thing would be?' The answer is simple. We read, watched and listened to everything to do with our industry. We read the business pages of every newspaper every day, subscribed to all the trade publications, listened to industry podcasts and kept an eye on everything.

 Hezi

This passion for learning always paid off. For example, we knew Apple's App Store was coming and instantly knew this would be great for Catch. So, we quickly briefed our developers to build an app for Catch and by the time the App Store launched, we were one of the first on it. It was such a simple, no-brainer thing to do, but because we were early to that tech party, Apple put our app on the 'trending' list and it stayed on the list for a year. Some would call that luck and we were definitely lucky on that front, but getting the app built, launching it quickly and moving into Apple's slipstream were critical elements in getting our app front and centre. A classic example of Mazal in action: location, timing and learning.

Interestingly, a lot of local retailers still do not have a functional app to complement their online shopping site. What a lost opportunity. Our mobile app has won many awards and is still one of the highest ranking apps in Apple's App Store. It was great for sales too, with roughly 70 per cent of our total transactions taken through a mobile phone. Customers clearly love this 'store-in-a-pocket' concept and apps are only going to get more popular.

Say 'yes' and work the rest out later

During 2010, our list of suppliers kept on growing. More household brands—such as Adidas, Cadbury, Sheridan and Canon—started appearing on Catch.

Perhaps our favourite newcomer was Antler, one of Australia's most respected luggage brands. After just one meeting with them, we got our first offer, a true clearance deal at a size that we had never seen before: 900 pallets. Forty semi-trailer loads of suitcases. OMG!

While we had moved into our 4000 m² Moorabbin warehouse a month earlier, the place was already close to being full. Business was still booming and orders were coming in from everywhere. What do we do with the Antler offer? Let it go? Take it up? The deal is great. We *can't* let it go. We had promised Antler we could help them with some clearance deals, but this deal was so massive we had nowhere to store the pallets. As luck would have it, across the road from us was a vacant warehouse with a 'For lease' sign on it. We didn't think twice. We immediately rented it for 12 months at $100 000 per year, paid Antler $1 million for the stock and accepted 900 pallets of the highest quality luggage you can imagine. That one Antler deal netted us $1 million in less than four months.

The lesson? When someone offers you a great deal, say 'yes' and work the rest out later.

That year—2010—was without a doubt the busiest, most stressful year of our lives. Everything we'd ever wanted was coming our way, but as always, we were working at full capacity and just kept taking on more and more. As they say, if you want something done, give it to a busy person.

Don't be afraid to make a profit

If there was ever an award for the most profitable Aussie e-commerce company, Catch would have won that award every year from 2006 to 2018. We launched Catch of the day in October 2006, and the business has been profitable every single day, week, month and year ever since.

There you go, we said it! We run a business and our aim is to sell a product or service that consumers love, employ a great team who love working for us, pay our taxes and then make money. Yes! We are also here to make money.

The pursuit of profit is not something that businesses or founders should hide. In fact, it is exactly the opposite: it is something that should be celebrated.

The reverse is also true: companies should be embarrassed and disappointed if they are making a loss, and should do everything they can to turn it around to become profitable.

We meet a lot of entrepreneurs seeking to raise funds at the seed stage before they have launched their business, before they have hired any employees and before they have built their minimum viable product (MVP). We think it's laughable that the founders consider the 'breakeven' point to be three or four years away from the launch date. Oh, how the world has changed!

In our early days, suppliers would often ask us, 'What's your margin?', or, in other words, 'If you buy a product for $100, what will you sell it for: $110, $130 or $200?' Traditional retailers generally expected a minimum set profit margin that varied according to the category they were operating in. Rigid and predictable.

We looked at it differently. Our aim was to buy the product for as little as possible, and sell it for as much as we could. For that to happen, three conditions had to be met:

- Could we move the product quickly?
- Could we create that 'wow' impact and impress our customers?
- Could we still offer customers the best prices in Australia?

If we could meet those conditions, we sometimes worked with margins as small as 5 per cent or margins as high as 400 per cent. When running a profitable business, making a nice profit margin and offering attractive deals are not mutually exclusive!

There's a famous line in retail:

'You make the money when you buy the goods, not when you sell the goods.'

If you are a retailer and you take out only one lesson from this book, that's it.

Meanwhile, our brand-new start-up—a fledgling little thing called Scoopon—was being bootstrapped out the back of the building, and we mean that literally.

Source: **Photo by Josh Robenstone**

CHAPTER 5

Idea by midnight, execute by midday

Here's the conversation that launched Scoopon—one of Australia's greatest disruptors of the service sector—and the story of how we moved quickly to get the idea to market. We both remember the discussion that took place at Nando's chicken shop* just after Hezi spotted Groupon, a US-based website that pioneered the group-buying concept.

Hezi

Check this website I spotted in the US. It's just like Catchoftheday but for services.

Gabby

We've seen a lot of shit lately, but this one is a winner.

---

* Gabby had the quarter chicken with peri peri sauce. Hezi had the burger and chips.

What Groupon did in the early days was group a bunch of buyers together to source a great offer from a local service provider. It was just like Catchoftheday, but for services. It worked on the same FOMO element of offering a great deal for a limited time on the premise the deal will most likely sell out.

By mid-2010, Catchoftheday was flying high. Things were going from strength to strength, so we could afford for Hezi to leave the room and take responsibility for the launch of Scoopon.

We lived by our motto, 'Idea by midnight, execute by midday', so by noon the next day, we were ready to go. Our mission? Let's turn Scoopon into the Catchoftheday of experiences and activities. There was no time to waste. After we agreed to pursue it, we spent the next hour brainstorming a great business name and settled on Scoopon (scoop + coupon. Genius!). The name was catchy, stood the test of time and it's (still) as good as ever.

Some of the services we sourced for Scoopon early on included deals like:

- a massage for $39 instead of $79

- a great meal at a local restaurant for $49 instead of $99

- discounted entry to an event, a conference or a park at 70 per cent less than the normal price.

It's hard to believe that this juggernaut, which would take the country by storm and spawn a plethora of copycats, began in a dilapidated shed out the back of the Catchoftheday offices. There was no room in the main office (it was already buzzing with 15 staff members) so this little 'side hustle' was banished to the back shed until it could pay its way. If WorkSafe inspectors had popped in, they'd have taken us to court. The room had no windows, no air and so few chairs that we had to wait for someone to get up to go to the toilet so we could sit down and check our emails at their desk.

WE LIVED BY OUR MOTTO,

'IDEA BY MIDNIGHT, EXECUTE BY MIDDAY'

SO BY NOON THE NEXT DAY, WE WERE READY TO GO.

How we launched Scoopon

 Hezi

I love the early days of a start-up: the buzz generated when you think you've come up with a great idea; the down you feel the next day when you start wondering if it's perhaps the dumbest idea in the world and someone tells you that it can't be done.

Catchoftheday was growing nicely and was very profitable, and while we could have afforded to hire teams to develop the sales channels for Scoopon, I wanted to run it lean and mean to see if the idea had legs before we invested more into it. I truly didn't know if the idea would work and I wanted to do my own homework to see what we were up against. The only way to do that was to pound the pavement, knock on doors and see what challenges awaited.

I reasoned that if I could make a dent and get a good reaction from the suppliers, then it meant that I could send a sales team into the field and have a reasonable expectation they'd succeed too. If I didn't do those hard yards at the start there would be no way of knowing if it was the business model, or the person selling it, that was flawed. Like Catch, sourcing suppliers for Scoopon was ridiculously hard, especially in those early weeks.

Here's what I did to get it off the ground.

I hired a junior graphic designer to create a replica of the Scoopon home page and I stuck it on an A3 piece of paper. (They call this an MVP now. I just called it a mock-up.) I got in my car and I drove around from car washes to massage parlours (the therapeutic ones, I may add!) in the area. I'd walk in, introduce myself as a sales rep for Scoopon, deliver my prepared sales pitch to the receptionist and promptly receive a polite but firm 'no'.

No matter how hard I tried and how many fancy marketing words I used, I couldn't get past the receptionist to speak to the owner.

I intentionally didn't introduce myself as the owner of the business, nor did I mention Catchoftheday, because in order to push through the door, I needed to see if the business model could stand on its own two feet.

Hezi representing the Scoopon brand.
Source: **Photo by Josh Robenstone**

After numerous knockbacks, I started to doubt whether this business model was going to work. It seemed no-one I spoke to could see the benefits of this product. I seriously contemplated giving it away but wanted to give it one more go. So, I decided to do something different. I flipped the pitch. Instead of spruiking how many eyeballs their business would get by being on the website, I said, 'We are looking for 500 massage vouchers for our members, and I'm scouting some different massage clinics in the area to see what's suitable. I've got $15 000 to spend.'

Boom! The floodgates opened.

Now I got put through instantly to the owner and the receptionist would go to great lengths to find the boss as no-one wanted to be the one who lost a $15 000 sale.

I'll never forget the first deal we featured when Scoopon launched in April 2010. I managed to convince an Endota Spa franchisee in South Melbourne to run a deal with Scoopon. I expected to sell 20 vouchers or, if we were lucky, maybe 50. In just three hours, we sold 873 massages for $40 each, half the normal price, making around $20 profit on each one. Do the maths. We made $17 000 on our first deal. We were all blown away. We had just discovered our next Catch! It was time to press the gas and hire a team.

I've always believed that when it comes to building a new business, you should never build the chimney before you build the house. Why would you? It's a risk and why waste money on something you haven't tested? Once we'd signed up 50 suppliers to the site across the three major cities of Melbourne, Sydney and the Gold Coast, I knew we had something, and only then could I justify investing in an expensive website and hiring teams of people.

Throughout our history we have always believed in hiring smart people with the right characteristics and attitude.

Jon Beros was one of them. He joined us early on and stayed with us, leading Scoopon until 2018. But hey, I'll hand the microphone over to Jon.

Jon

I first heard about Scoopon when Catchoftheday issued a media release announcing the impending launch of the site. I was sold on the idea as soon as I heard it, and after searching the net for contact details, I was sitting with Hezi and Gabby later that week.

Jon Beros steered the ship that was Scoopon through the stormy seas of setting up the site in Australia.

My job was to build a team and, luckily, I received an open cheque book with a mandate to start hiring immediately. I could see how they'd made Catchoftheday such a success. These guys moved quickly. We started with five people: three in sales, one copywriter and one in admin. They all sat in a dusty little office at the back of the main office. We had no idea what to expect, no manual on how to build it, and no expectation of how big it would become, but we had a healthy dose of excitement and optimism that this was an idea that could work.

My directions were clear: build it fast but profitably— which is exactly how I liked to roll.

Our first task was to create a sales strategy that would enable us to educate the merchants on how it worked. The business model was pretty easy to understand:

- The merchant pays nothing upfront.
- They offer an exclusive deal.

- We market their offer to a huge audience (and drive sales to their website at the same time).

- We take a commission for our efforts and the merchant services the customer.

In essence, it's an advertising campaign where the merchant only pays for each customer successfully acquired. How's that for a win-win?

Our pitch to the merchants was equally simple. We used the opening line 'We are from Scoopon, a sister site of Catchoftheday, Australia's number-one shopping site'. That one-liner opened doors for us in a big way.

Just as Catchoftheday was rewriting retail norms, Scoopon was doing it in the vertical services industry, while flipping traditional marketing on its head.

The name of the game was scale. We had to scale fast and we were glad we did because within a few weeks of launching we had almost 80 competitors pop up out of nowhere, many of them with serious backing behind them. Cudo (owned by Channel Nine), Spreets (owned by Channel Seven), Our Deal (Channel Ten), plus LivingSocial, jumponit, Zoupon and dozens more like them all piled in, hoping to grab a slice of the pie.

Unlike Catchoftheday, which had high barriers to entry (funds to buy large volumes of product, space to warehouse it, logistics teams to manage it, and so on) almost anyone could enter this burgeoning industry. All you needed was a website that could print a coupon, a sales person to sort out the deals and a phone, and you had yourself a Daily Deal business. The market saturation was completely unsustainable, but we had a point of difference, and a valuable one at that. We had the backing of Catchoftheday, Australia's most successful home-grown start-up. We'd just won the Hitwise award and been named as Australia's number-one most visited shopping site. As a result, we had access to the massive Catchoftheday database of more than half a million price-savvy customers, all hungry for a good deal. We were sitting on a customer database goldmine and it helped us leapfrog to the top of the pack.

How fast did we find success? Immediately. Here's the blog we used to tell our suppliers how good we were, how fast we were growing and why they should work with us.

What a huge month it was for Catch!

May 4, 2010

Wow! April has gone with the wind, and what a month it was for us! Here are some of the highlights.

Scoopon.com.au was launched in the only way we know how to launch things—with a massive bang.

In effect we started a whole new category in Australia, of selling services and experiences with the Catchoftheday twist: 24 hours and it's gone.

For a site that's not even a month old, you'll have to agree that we uncovered a real gem here. Check out some of the 'Scoopons' we sold:

- 1474 indoor paintball coupons
- 684 half price Luna Park tickets
- 873 half price massages at Endota Spa
- 3470 dinner cruises on Sydney Harbour.

These are some pretty spectacular numbers!

If you are a supplier of anything from sporting tickets to accommodation to a restaurant or bungee jumping, get in touch with us and let us put some bums on seats for you, with no upfront commitment. It's a win-win.

Grab a copy of this month's *BRW* to see us coolly placed at #3 in the annual 100 Fast Starters list. Thank you, Australia! Our phenomenal growth would not have been possible without your tremendous word-of-mouth support! We couldn't ask for anything better.

Sales are skyrocketing. Last week we sold a stupidly high number of GPS units (4600 to be exact), making sure that no person in Australia will get lost ever again.

Last week we re-launched our wine.catchoftheday.com.au, and as you may have noticed our buyers must have been drunk when deciding on the sale price. 4000 cases of Wolf Blass were sold in less than 21 hours, which kept our warehouse guys really busy stepping on grapes for the whole weekend! Expect the party to continue every Wednesday at midday with another release of an unbeatable drop.

And while we're all here ... are you receiving our SOS emails? What's an SOS email? I'm glad you asked. It means, Subscriber Only Special!

Every night, we send an email out around 6 pm, with an unbelievable offer for a product that we just don't have enough of to share with the rest of the country. If you are not receiving them, you are certainly missing out. Subscribe here!

And here's another small incentive. Tomorrow midday we will send an email with a $10 Catchoftheday gift voucher; I think this is one newsletter that you don't want to miss out on. Full details will be in tomorrow's email.

Yours sincerely

The Catch Team

Clap for yourself and others will join in the applause

By now you'll know that we were always prepared to shout from the rooftops about how good we were, how much we were selling and who we were working with. It made good business sense to do so. If *we* didn't tell everyone, who would? Looking back, our biggest regret is we didn't shout louder! After all, we had a lot to shout about.

Our blogs and emails were key planks in our communications strategy and they played a big role in helping us achieve the word of mouth that accelerated our results. The Catch database had half a million customers on it so we leveraged it to showcase our new Scoopon business. We already had their trust so asking them to try this new service was an easy way to gain traction. As a sales communication channel the blog was unbeatable. It had huge engagement rates and our customers loved it because we wrote as we spoke: frankly, honestly (sometimes too honestly!) and quickly. We didn't use fancy words, or clever copy techniques. We used simple language that everyone could understand and made it punchy so they'd read through to the end.

Consistency was important—our blog went out once a month and was full of attention-grabbing nibbles that the customer, supplier or media might find interesting. There was something for everyone! Staff news, sales highlights, new deals, records broken, awards we'd won … Our blogs were always upbeat, motivational and super positive, and highlighted the FOMO element. The key message we wanted to communicate was, 'If you are not shopping with us, you are really missing out'.

We always believed that you need to promote yourself, and we did a lot of that—and these blogs helped us do it exponentially. You need to start clapping for yourself first, and then everyone else will join in the applause.

Right time, right place, right idea

Again, we managed to launch a business that hit the market just at the right place and at the right time. Scoopon was firing on all cylinders. Merchants were coming onboard left, right and centre and we were even turning many away. Customers couldn't get enough of the deals, and who could blame them, when we were the first to offer them a half price massage or a half price dinner. These kinds of deals are common now (because of Scoopon) but back then, it was ground breaking.

The media loved what we were doing, and a strategy of amazing deals and plenty of PR helped lay the rail tracks that would help us build a brand known Australia wide.

By late 2010 our little headquarters were bursting at the seams so we moved into the Catchoftheday head office in Moorabbin. Compared to our little tin shed, we felt like we'd landed in Google's headquarters. We had enough space for everyone to have a desk and room to grow. Luxury! Catch had 20 office staff, Scoopon had 15 and we all celebrated the move by spending the weekend setting up the office for what we felt would last for at least another five years. We lasted one.

The launch of Scoopon Travel

Jon

The creation of Scoopon Travel came about when we received a phone call from the Portsea Hotel. Until this point Scoopon sold coupons for restaurant meals, day spas, sports activities and events. Our average price point was around $50. My colleague called to me across the room: 'Jon, it's the Portsea Hotel. They want to run an accommodation offer on the site. Can we do that?' Now, there are times in business when key moments stay with you—and this was one of them. I remember everyone in the room stopped what they were doing and we all kind of looked at each other, silently wondering why a hotel was calling us. Being the decisive leader that I am, my response was along the lines of, 'Shit, I don't know, can we?' I recovered in time to say, 'Just say yes, and we'll work the rest out later'.

After getting our heads around signing up a hotel and trying to figure out how the logistics and redemptions would work, we launched the deal on the site not long after. We had a maximum of 800 room nights to sell and I was hoping we would sell enough and not embarrass ourselves, which in my mind was at least one! The offer went live and within four hours we had sold out!

Scoopon revolutionised the way restaurants, hotels and other services marketed themselves in Australia.

As they say, 'From little things, big things grow', and soon, our travel category made up 50 per cent of Scoopon's revenue. That one hotel deal led to the creation of a dedicated high-end travel site called bonvoyage.com.au. That then merged with the market leader Luxuryescapes.com.au to become one of Australia's most successful travel deal sites, and subsequently became the second major exit for the group.

It's hard to describe how big 2010 was for us. This blog, which we sent to all our customers, comes close.

Hi there,

It's been a momentous year at Catchoftheday and Scoopon.

Many milestones have been reached and records shattered. We'd like to thank you for the success of this humble site because now we are officially Australia's no.1 department store and the most talked about shopping site in the country.

It's your word of mouth and loyalty that is driving all this forward. In return you can expect even bigger things from us next year. Every year the catches keep getting better and that won't change in 2011.

Scoopon.com.au was launched in early April, and it is now the undisputed leader in the daily coupon scene. Scoopon now employs 25 people and is looking to continue the growth in years to come.

Scoopon sells discounted coupons for services and fun things to do around your city. Last week alone Scoopon sold over 20 000 coupons, saving Australians over $2 million. Wow!

The site was launched simply by announcing it to our ever-growing database of 550 000 members. Imagine what will happen when we start advertising next year!

We know you all love numbers and stats, so here are some interesting figures from 2010.

Awards:

- *BRW* Fast Starters: no.3 Australia wide
- ANZ *BRW* Finalist: Fastest growing Australian private company
- Deloitte Technology Leadership Award
- Deloitte 500 fastest growing technology companies in Asia–Pacific
- Best Father award: from my daughters on Father's Day.

The Stats:

- Membership has grown to 550 000 members. 50 000 of them joined in November alone. Our members join simply because they like our deals and tell their friends about them.
- Sales revenue has grown by 230 per cent this financial year. Good luck to all the old fashion retailers with their 2.1 per cent annual growth.
- We receive around 100 000 unique visitors every day. On massive days we can have as many as 150 000 people logging in.
- 80 per cent of our visitors visit us more than four times a week (because they want to!)
- Over 8000 Mossimo branded apparel items were snapped up in 24 hours
- Over 7000 sets of pearls were sold in a day
- 10 000 pillows were sold in 5 hours
- 4000 pairs of shoes ran out the door just as quick
- 140 000 Supermax razors gone in a day

- 15 000 Sennheiser headphones—boom!
- 70 000+ grocery items are sold

and the list goes on.

Catch will also be launching two new sister sites in fresh new categories next year. More details to come!

Every day at noon it's always heart-warming to see thousands of you online and eagerly awaiting the next Catch. It's what keeps us working this hard, and we'll be going even further next year. What else can we say? You love us and we love you back.

Merry Christmas and Happy New Year, from all of us at Catchoftheday.com.au! Drive carefully and celebrate responsibly!

Gabby, Hezi and the Catch Team

Apply for awards

Everyone loves a winner, and everyone wants to work for, deal with and buy from one. So, how do you become one? One way is to win awards, and even if you don't win, being nominated is almost as good.

Awards helped us achieve a number of goals all at once. They created awareness of our brand, which attracted more customers, which generated more revenue.

We have won many awards over the years—Best Australian Shopping Site, Best App, Customer Choice, Most Visited Shopping Site—too many to mention them all. Funnily enough, the one we remember the most is our first one, the Smart Company Smart50 Awards in 2009. We came 38th but we didn't care! We were in the running and that got us noticed.

Applying for awards takes time and effort and don't forget that the companies running the awards are actually businesses themselves, making a profit through application fees and award ceremonies. With this in mind, it's worth noting that the chances that you will win the same award two years in a row are pretty slim, as the organisers need to spread them around, but winning one puts you in good stead to win another, different award.

When you do win an award, tell everyone. Scream it from the rooftops. Let the whole world know how good your business is. Your award should be displayed everywhere from email signatures and social media to your website homepage—everywhere.

Who's going to stop me?

When you're up against the big boys of retail, as we were, you have to act and appear bigger than you really are—not just to convince the competitors, or the customers (or even the media) that you are a force to be reckoned with, but to convince yourself!

We love category killer companies such as JB Hi-Fi and Chemist Warehouse because they have the guts to clearly state what they stand for: price. When you walk into Chemist Warehouse you will see a sign like this:

Is this Australia's cheapest chemist?

We love that kind of statement! It is ambiguous, yet so effective.

In the early days we also used grandiose claims that told the world we existed. We started with lines like:

We sell a product every 25 seconds.

We got bolder.

We sell a product every 7 seconds.

And bolder.

We sell a product every second!

Other one-liners that worked well were:

We are Australia Post's No. 1 client.

We have 200 000 visitors come to see us every day. That is more than Chadstone gets at Christmas!

We will be a billion-dollar company in 3 years.

These were true statements. We knew what we stood for. We were discounters. We were proud discounters. In any case, who's going to stop you from saying it? What's your '25 seconds'? Find it and stand out from the crowd.

We celebrated the end of the year by taking our staff of 60 and their partners on a cruise around Melbourne's Port Phillip Bay. It's amazing to think that so much had been achieved by such a small team. It was clear we were doing something very special.

And from a distance we were also being watched by a whole new group of people: investors.

CHAPTER 6
Catch us if you can

When we started Catchoftheday we were content to go it alone and we weren't actually looking for an investor. We had built a good-looking business, won a bunch of awards and shown enough entrepreneurial talent for people to become interested in us. By early 2010, we'd started receiving a lot of interest from local and international venture capitalists, private and public companies, high net worth families and wealthy individuals. Companies such as Insight Venture Partners, Sequoia, Yahoo7, Level Equity, Bessemer, Intel Capital and others lined up to court us, valuing our business at $50 million one day, $80 million a month later. Wait! Do I hear $120 million? Is $150 million your final offer? Going, going … It was going nuts. We dated a lot of suitors. It was an honour to be invited for lunches and coffees with some very influential parties that we had only read about in magazines.

However, as the meetings progressed, we became more confused about why we were on the investor dating market in the first place. Our business was quite profitable, and we had the funds required for our projected growth. What were we actually wanting?

Still, we kept our minds open and were flattered that this little business, which had started just five years earlier, was now being courted by companies that had invested in Facebook, Apple and other unicorns. The upshot? We turned them all down and waited for our Prince Charming to arrive.

To be honest, despite the fact we had doubled sales every eight months and were fielding sophisticated investment offers from some experienced investors, we were not experts in finance at all and these fancy Sand Hill Road types were incredibly intimidating. Hand on heart, we didn't even know what CFO meant! We're not kidding. At this stage, we still had one book-keeper and a part-time accountant (Hi Vitalyi!). It was a lean operation. Looking back, we should have hired professional advisers earlier. We're big believers now in hiring the best advice you can, but back then, we didn't know enough to know what we were missing out on. These days, there's so much support for start-ups: incubators, accelerators, angel investors, mentors, grants and more. We had none of that, but we didn't know any different.

The pressure was intensifying. We were being inundated with financial offers from the world's smartest money people at one of the busiest times in the history of Catch—with Groupon, the Goliath of group deals, breathing down our neck. We needed help to sift through the offers, and we went searching for it.

Here's a snippet of the email we sent to the smartest adviser we knew at the time:

> Hi D,
>
> We need your help. Our weakest link right now is on the financial side of the business. We're getting a lot of approaches and hearing terms like floating, board of directors, CFO, P/E ratio, and lots of other terms and would like someone external to come in help us make sense of it all and guide us to the next level. Is this something you can help us with?

We needed his advice because when it came to big business, all is not what it seems and without careful guidance you can make mistakes. Costly ones. We nearly made one by underestimating a young man called Lee Fixel from Tiger Global. He was one of the many venture capitalists who contacted us. We checked to see if he had an online presence (he didn't), so we basically ignored him.

The Tiger who came to tea

 Gabby

Through good luck and my wife's insistence, we took a holiday to Bali and bumped into Jason Lenga, one of the top executives at recruitment giant seek.com.au, in our hotel's foyer. Mazal was at work again. Location, timing and learning.

Jason told us Seek had just taken investment from Tiger Global for its websites in Brazil and China and spoke highly of Lee Fixel. Little did we know, but Tiger Global, and in particular Lee, were the most respected and successful venture capitalists in the world. He also said they had invested in e-commerce giants such as Flipkart and JD.com and that if they invest in you, they will not seek to corporatise the business or change the culture. Considering our corporate attire rarely involved more than shorts and thongs, this was music to our ears.

We made contact with Lee again, invited him to Melbourne and organised to have dinner at Rockpool at Melbourne's Crown Casino, the first time we'd stepped foot in this flashy establishment. We brought Anees with us, who was by now well and truly an integral member of our team. He balanced us out and often cast the final vote if we couldn't agree on something.

We knew what figure we were looking for from Lee. One hundred and fifty million dollars had been the top valuation we'd received from other investors, so we plucked $200 million out of the air as our desired valuation and decided that if we got that, we'd sign, and if we didn't, we wouldn't. The worst-case scenario? We'd get a nice $200 steak dinner courtesy of Tiger Global.

Lee turned out to be the nicest, and smartest, 31-year-old guy we'd ever met. During dinner, he tossed us a question that we hesitated to answer truthfully for fear it would kill the deal. The question? 'Tell me guys, if Gabby and Hezi got run over by a bus tomorrow, what would happen to Catchoftheday?' We answered it the only way we knew how—honestly—and admitted that without us, there would be no business. He appreciated our candour, and then proceeded to ask us what price we were seeking. We were so nervous we couldn't even bring ourselves to verbalise the words. Fortunately, we had Anees there and his job was to deliver the news. Anees dropped the magic figure: two hundred million.

We watched Lee like a hawk, trying to stay calm and nonchalant. Lee put down his steak knife, took a sip of his red wine, looked at each one of us, smiled and replied with one word:

'Deal'.

We hugged, ordered another bottle of wine and celebrated into the night.

Life at Catchoftheday was never going to be the same again.

Life, in fact, was never going to be the same again.

Signing the Tiger deal. Life was never going to be the same again.

Catches

1   If you haven't succeeded yet, don't give up. Success can come at any time, at any age.

2   If the front door and back door are closed, try the 'third' door.

3   Don't hold your cards too close to your chest. Talk about your ideas, let others know what you're doing and the idea will progress much faster.

4   People aren't out to steal your ideas. The winner will be the one with the best execution.

5   Don't let your passion for a product cloud your commercial judgement. Give the customers what *they* want, not what *you* want.

6   Fail fast. Learn your lessons early, and get on with it.

7   Don't take 'no' for an answer.

8   Ask questions, and if you don't get the answer you want, ask again, ask another person or ask at a different time.

9   When you're presented with an opportunity, just say 'yes' and work the rest out later.

10 Be first to market if you can. If you can't be first, be second. If you're not in the top three, it will be a lot harder.

11 When you're starting out and funds are tight, hire allrounders willing to do a bit of everything.

12 Be frugal with spending, especially in the early days, and especially with investor money.

13 Don't spend money you don't have.

14 Don't spend on things that don't make a material difference to your business.

15 Own your own platform, if you can.

16 Don't rely on one product, business arm or sales channel. Spread the risk.

17 Take responsibility for growing your own database because whoever owns the customer owns the gold.

18 Your idea does not need to be original in order to be successful.

19 Choose a business name that will stand the test of time. Try not to name your business after a person, street or suburb.

20 Don't wait for perfection before you launch ideas, logos, websites, products or businesses.

21 Every minute you procrastinate costs you money.

22 Focus on releasing the features that make the product work, and release quickly. All the 'nice-to-haves' can come later.

23 You're only as good as your last deal.

24 To niche or not to niche? At some point, you'll need to decide. Whichever way you go, there'll be risk.

25 The best way to make a person want something is to tell them they can't have it.

26 A 'Sold Out' sign is the best word-of-mouth recommendation you can get. As said by my friend, real estate agent Phillip Kingston from Garypeer.com.au.

27 For FOMO to work, you need to have a high-quality product. People may queue for crap once, but not twice.

28 You can't please all of the people all of the time. Choose the people you want to please, and work hard to 'surprise and delight' them.

29 You don't get lucky sitting on the sofa with your arms crossed. Get out there and make it happen.

30 Timing is everything.

31 To build a business, you need to be out and about. Socialise, attend events, travel. Circulating increases your chances of being in the right place at the right time.

32 Knowledge is power. Read, watch and listen to everything related to your industry.

33 Immerse yourself in your niche. Knowing your category allows you to spot an opportunity the moment it comes your way.

34 Know what problem you solve.

35 Great buyers are born, not made, but you can learn how to be a better one.

36 If you're not good at something, hire someone who is.

37 Curiosity powers creativity. Great entrepreneurs always ask 'why?'

38 Be an honest person, and do the right thing. It's the quickest way to build trust.

39 If you're a jerk, the word will quickly get around.

40 Build a relationship with your supplier. Everyone prefers to deal with a friend rather than just a faceless executive.

41 Pay your suppliers on time. Even better, pay them ahead of time.

42	Leave money on the table.
43	Business should not be transaction driven but relationship driven.
44	Business is not just about the first deal. It's about all the deals that come after, and the lifelong relationship that is built up over that time.
45	In business, everyone has to win: the supplier, the retailer and the customer.
46	A relationship can only continue and thrive if both parties are happy over the long term.
47	Don't screw your suppliers over. Ever.
48	People do business with people they like.
49	Don't get down to business too quickly. Start your meetings with five minutes of random chit chat.
50	You can't fall in love unless you go on a date. Relationships are best built face to face. Meet in person.
51	Don't deal with conflict over email or the phone. It's too easy to misconstrue feelings. Make the effort to meet over a coffee, or go for a walk.
52	Don't get angry over email. Count to 100 and then respond. You will almost always be thankful you didn't act in haste.
53	Don't leave voicemails. No-one listens to them anymore. If you don't get the person, hang up and ring back.
54	Be funny. Crack jokes. It relaxes people. 'Funny is money.'
55	Never close a door. Once closed, they're very hard to open. Work hard to keep them open.
56	Say 'thank you' to those who helped you get where you are.

57 Turn challenges and setbacks into opportunities. The best ideas arise from solving 'unsolvable' problems.

58 Necessity is the mother of invention.

59 Create a hard-copy, one-page flyer that summarises your business and take it with you to meetings. You never know when you might need it.

60 If you can, commit to and pay for goods at the time of purchase and you'll always get the best deal.

61 Nothing beats a word-of-mouth recommendation from a friend or a workmate.

62 Get a whiteboard. Online tools are great but when everyone can see the bigger picture at once, you'll get better results.

63 Try new ideas. Even if they don't work, you'll know what not to do next time.

64 Not all recessions are bad.

65 Even with the best business idea in the world, if no-one knows about you, you've got nothing.

66 Invest in PR. Learn how to do it yourself, or pay a professional to do it for you.

67 PR builds credibility. Credibility builds trust. Trust is everything.

68 When the media come calling, make yourself available.

69 Work hard to get on TV. The effort is worth it.

70 Be excited when a journalist calls. If you're not excited about your business story, why should the journalist be?

71 Provide the journalist with a package of data, images and stories. It will help them write a better story about you.

72 If you're going on TV, wear a branded T-shirt so people are visually reminded of who you represent.

73 Preparation is everything. Rehearse your script well before the cameras start rolling.

74 Be consistent with your PR efforts. Successful PR is a marriage, not a one-off date.

75 Be accessible to journalists. Give them your mobile and let them know they can contact you at short notice.

76 To take big risks you need to start by taking little risks. Risk-taking gets easier with repetition.

77 Being an entrepreneur means you need to get comfortable being uncomfortable.

78 You need to spend money to make money.

79 If you want something done, give it to a busy person.

80 Don't be rigid with setting margins. Buy the product for as little as possible, and sell it for as much as you can.

81 Making a nice profit margin and offering attractive deals are not mutually exclusive.

82 You make the money when you buy the goods, not when you sell the goods.

83 Speed of execution is everything. If you have a great idea at midnight, execute it by midday.

84 Create an MVP so you can show people what you're doing. A flyer, slide deck, mock-up, white paper—have something to show prospective buyers.

85 Don't take rejection personally.

86 Develop a high tolerance for humiliation.

87 If your sales pitch isn't working, try another one. If that doesn't work, find a new one. Keep trying until it works.

88 Don't waste too much money on a new idea before testing it. Why build the chimney before you build the house?

89 Hire smart people with the right characteristics and attitude.

90 If your customers and suppliers don't understand your business model, it's too complicated.

91 Focus on scale. If you can't, you'll be overtaken by those who can.

92 Clap for yourself, and the others will join in the applause.

93 Shout from the rooftops how successful you are. If you don't tell the world how good you are, who will?

94 Use your blogs and email newsletters to tell your customers about your successes.

95 If you're going to send out email newsletters, be consistent about when you send them.

96 Apply for awards. Everyone loves a winner, and everyone wants to be associated with one.

97 If you don't win the award, don't worry. If at first you don't succeed, try again.

98 Applying for awards takes time and effort, but it's worth it. Make the time.

99 When you do win an award, tell everyone. Display the icon on your email signatures, social media and website. Put it everywhere.

100 If the business does well, reward those who helped you get there.

101 Act and appear bigger than you really are.

102 Travel while you're young. Take a year off after school or university and explore the world. We didn't and we regret it.

103   Have the guts to clearly state what you stand for. Be grandiose and let the world know you exist.

104   If you're searching for investment, be clear about why you want it and what you're prepared to give up for it.

105   Don't take the first investment offer that comes your way.

106   If you don't have the answers, or even the questions, ask for advice. People are often very happy to give you help if you have the courage to ask for it.

107   Don't test your product concept on friends. They'll always say, 'It's a great idea!' Test it on your target market and ask them to pay for it.

108   If you get asked difficult questions, answer them honestly. People will appreciate your candour.

Part II
Ramping up

CHAPTER 7
Time to scale

'No offence guys, you've done a great job to get the business this far, but now we need some rock stars to take it up a notch!' said Lee Fixel, the man from Tiger Global.

What he really meant was:

Let's bring in some more experienced people who've run a business many times this size to help you run this show.

Tiger Global had just invested $80 million for a 40 per cent share of our business, and Lee was here on their behalf to make sure we delivered on it. It's not uncommon for venture capitalists to surround the founders with people of their choice, and this situation was no different. They believed that a CEO and a stronger management team (with corporate and public company experience) would always be a safer bet than two founders with no real track record of running a corporate business.

Prior to their investment in May 2011, the Catch and Scoopon businesses were run by a management team of Gabby, Hezi and Anees, backed up by Vijay, Catch's first employee, who took care of logistics and operations. None of us carried any titles, and if there were major strategic decisions to be made about hiring, firing, marketing or negotiations, we all had a say. None of us had executive assistants or highly paid advisers. We still checked all our own emails, booked our own meetings and thrived on the adrenaline of making it all work. We were a real team. We ran what we considered to be a small business. It was a fast-growing small business, and a very profitable one at that, but we treated it as a small business.

With the arrival of Tiger Global, all that changed.

This influx of venture capital came with added pressure. We were being watched and they expected us to deliver. The message? Scale. Grow. Now!

Within months, we'd gone from not knowing what a CFO is, to forking out $2 million in annual salaries on hiring a raft of C-level guys: CEO, CFO, CIO, CMO (and a whole bunch of other Cs). We also formed a board and started having monthly board meetings—or 'bored' meetings, as we called them!

So much was happening so quickly that we needed to keep everyone informed, including our suppliers. They've always been part of our three-way wedding (Catch-supplier-customer) so we needed to bring them along on the journey. Remember, without suppliers there is no business! Here's how we announced our $80 million investment to them.

Dear Supplier,

We have some very significant news.

An investment consortium of Tiger Global Management (investors in Facebook, Zynga and LinkedIn), James Packer's Consolidated Press Holdings, Andrew Bassat from SEEK and Glenn Poswell from Gannet Capital have just acquired a minority stake in our business and become our partners.

The deal values our company at $200 million, making it the largest investment in the Australian e-commerce sector to date.

It was a tough decision, but when James Packer agreed to throw in discounted parking at the casino to all staff, we knew it was a deal we couldn't refuse.

We're sure many of you have some burning questions to ask. We will attempt to pre-empt as many of them as possible.

Q: Will we be still working wearing shorts and thongs?

A: Absolutely. In fact, anyone seen wearing a tie will be fired immediately.

Q: Will I be dealing with some big executive?

A: Absolutely not. No-one is coming in to sit over our heads and monitor how we run this business. We've tricked them into thinking we know what we are doing so they're going to trust our 'unique' way of getting things done.

You will continue dealing with the same buyers including Gabby, Anees, Kalman and Marissa.

Q: What's on Catch tomorrow?

A: No idea! See, nothing's changed! Keep emailing us these offers and we will keep making our million-dollar decisions within five minutes!

Q: So, nothing is going to change?

A: Well, nothing much ... except ... we'll be moving into a massive new building and it's enormous. In simple terms we are looking at around four times our current office space. The warehouse is also four times bigger, meaning no more lame 'Warehouse Clearance' sales and much faster packing. Oh, and we should be launching another two websites (Mumgo and Grocery Run), which should give many of you the opportunity to sell us more stock in more segments.

There is also the small matter of the suitcases full of cash now available to support new technology investments, a couple of acquisitions of other similar minded internet start-ups and a few media and advertising campaigns to top it off.

Let's not forget that with this deal we are also in some very fine company indeed, with not just financial resources but an equally casual dress sense, passion for the internet, huge experience, knowledge, contacts and a shared hunger to break records in this fast-growing scene.

To wrap things up, we still own most of the business and will be staying put working hard to make it even bigger and better.

Thank you for your continued support over the last five years. Online shopping is just starting now, and we are looking forward to leading this market into the future.

Hold on tight, it's going to be a fun ride!

Don't forget to email us now. We are in a good mood today, use it to your advantage!

Yours,

Gabby, Hezi and The Catch Team

Within 18 months of Tiger Global's investment, we'd mushroomed from 100 employees to 300. What the f$#@! Let us repeat that: within 18 months, we'd grown from 100 to 300 staff members. How did we grow so quickly? More on that later, but being featured on the front cover of *BRW* didn't hurt. That was a super proud day for us. Here we were, two guys who started with a stall at the markets, now on the cover of Australia's premier business magazine! The magazine is gone now, but we're still here.

This media coverage didn't just create great memories for us, it created great momentum for the business, which enabled us to grow quickly. More media meant more customers, which meant more deals, which meant more sales, which led to greater exposure. The cycle of success was in full swing. Business was already booming and then it just exploded. The warehouse was packed, the offers were pouring in, and people were working to capacity. And while growth is great, it created problems.

THE BIG FAT GREEK DISASTER: WHAT IT MEANS FOR OUR ECONOMY

BRW.

Know which wa

CARBON PRICE CONUNDRUM
How it will impact your business
LIFE AFTER THE WIRE
Telstra moves beyond copper
SURVIVAL AS A SUBSIDIARY
Tips for after the takeover
SMART TALK: RICHARD BRANSON
When to dump whinging customers

CATCH OF THE DAY
HOW WE GOT $80M FROM PACKER & CO

Gabby and Hezi Leibovich, founders of Catch of the Day

July 14-20, 2011
$7.95 (inc.GST)
www.brw.com.au
ISSN 07277458

The *BRW* cover story documented how and why Tiger Global and some of Australia's wealthiest families invested in Catchoftheday.
***Source*: © Fairfax Media**

Growing pains

People often ask us what the biggest challenge in building this business has been, and to be honest, we can pin it down to a single factor: 'growing pains'. Here are our yearly sales results.

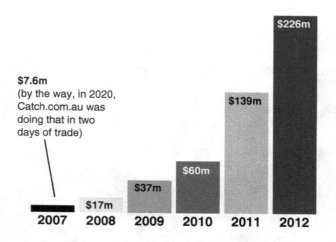

We have pretty much doubled our business every single year since launching, which generally meant doubling our team size, doubling the number of parcels dispatched, needing to find and invent new processes to accommodate the growth, and moving four offices and four warehouses at the same time.

Growing pains are never easy, but it's a fact of life for disruptors. The upside to this pain was we had good people, solid infrastructure and streamlined processes to support what we were experiencing, and we were having a lot of fun! Do you know what was the hardest part? Moving. Who likes moving house? No-one. Times it by a million and you get the size of the headache. It's not just the time-consuming tasks of dealing with real estate agents, inspecting new properties, restructuring finances and revising all the corporate collateral to reflect the new location. It's also the *physical* act of moving and the logistics of relocating hundreds of staff, tonnes of warehouse machinery, thousands of boxes of stock and the requisite clean-up of the premises that made the moving process so exhausting.

So, in mid 2012 we reluctantly decided to geographically separate the business into two parts. Why? Both businesses grew so fast that we simply ran out of office space and, in particular, we needed more storage and warehousing capacity. Gabby and the teams of Catchoftheday and Grocery Run moved to another, bigger office/warehouse in Braeside (How big? 16 000 m² big—the size of the Melbourne Cricket Ground!) and Hezi and the Scoopon team, still growing fast, stayed put at the Moorabbin office/warehouse.

Every start-up wants to scale up as quickly as possible, and we were no different. With the pressure from Tiger Global, we knew that we had to do something innovative to achieve it, and we knew it would come at a cost because at critical junctures like this, it becomes physically impossible to achieve growth without making major structural change.

This is how we did it.

Until mid 2012, Catchoftheday was all about a catch of a day: selling a single deal in high volumes, creating a lot of buzz and doing it all again the next day. It was a winning formula that propelled us to the top of the online retail leader board, all in six years. Selling one deal a day in large volumes had allowed us to streamline our packing process. It's pretty simple to pack 3000 of a single item into 3000 postage bags, and then load them onto the Australia Post truck. These logistics were a piece of cake compared to what we were about to implement. Looking back, oh how we miss those days of the single deal!

But with few suppliers who could meet our need to supply one product in the quantities we needed (which was thousands) for each deal, we sadly had to say goodbye to our single-deal-a-day format. It was not a decision we made lightly. To scale, we moved to an 'events' format, which brought with it the potential for growth, but all manner of headaches too.

In short, 'events' were Catchoftheday deals on steroids.

Each event had anything from one to 1000 products available for sale each day, and each event was dedicated to a single brand or theme. The deals were still time limited, and the event started and ended at given times throughout the day.

While the event format enabled us to offer a lot more deals on any given day, and increase our revenue, it also created a series of operational and financial challenges we had never faced before.

For a start, our previous fulfilment process of packing one product into one bag had now become a highly complex task involving thousands of different products in millions of combinations going to hundreds of thousands of people. It was complicated. That wasn't the only challenge. We now needed:

- more storage rooms to handle the increase in received goods

- more packing staff in our warehouses to manage the goods

- more photographers and copywriters to promote the events

- more IT people to handle the growing demands and loads of a heavier website

- even more finance teams to handle the increase in accounts

… and much more money to purchase a greater range of goods.

And if this wasn't enough to manage, we added four new sites in 2012:

- Grocery Run
- Mumgo
- Vinomofo
- EatNow

… to our existing sites of Catchoftheday and Scoopon.

We hung up this airline arrival-style board in our foyer to showcase when our new brands and websites started (landed).

In addition to moving to the massive new warehouse in Braeside, we opened a larger logistics centre (23 000 m², even bigger than the other one) in the suburb of Truganina, 28 kilometres west of Melbourne. Add to that the opening of new offices for Scoopon in every major capital city around the country and voilà!

That was the short version of how the hell we managed to mushroom from 100 workers to 300 workers in a year and a bit (and then 400 one year after that) and how we suddenly found ourselves running a not-so-small business anymore.

CHAPTER 8
Running fast

You may have noticed we slipped in that small matter of adding four new websites in one year to the business. We could dedicate an entire book to how we built those four start-ups but here's the short version.

The launch of Grocery Run

Kalman Polak had worked in various retail stores, including Panasales and The Good Guys, so when a buying role came up at our short-lived bricks and mortar store, we were thrilled to offer him the role.

Over the next 18 months, Kalman started spotting possibilities for future growth for the business. He moved from the shop floor to joining the Catch of the Day buying team. And at one of these meetings he pitched the idea of selling groceries online as no one was doing it. We loved the idea and GroceryRun was born.

How Grocery Run Started

Exciting, ground-breaking and successful, Grocery Run was a booming business that shook the Australian retail industry and gave the Australian market a new way to shop. Here's Kalman to tell you the story.

Kalman

It all began in 2011, when I was trying to think of something the Aussie consumer needed. I came up with the idea of trying to sell discounted grocery deals online. I thought it could have real potential.

When Gabby and Hezi gave me the green light, I proceeded to do what they had been doing all along: sourcing great products at great prices. I just started doing it in the grocery space. I began by asking suppliers a simple question: 'Do you have any excess stock to sell?' The suppliers I contacted definitely did. I chose the best 50 brands I could get and bought between 200 and 1000 units of each, ranging from toiletries and cleaning supplies to pantry products.

We put all the products online and created an event for Catchoftheday called Grocery Run. The response was phenomenal. We launched at midday and by 5pm we'd sold out of everything. We tested it out on the Catch site for a while and after making $1 million in sales—and more than $200 000 in gross profit in just two days—we quickly realised that Grocery Run deserved a site of its own.

Despite the reputation Catch had built over the previous six years, I went through all the same issues the guys had gone through trying to get Catch and Scoopon off the ground. In short: brands and suppliers were risk averse and no-one wanted to be the first to do anything (except us!). But we eventually wore down the grocery suppliers and snared some great brands. We launched the stand-alone GroceryRun. com.au website in September 2011 and in two weeks gained 271 000 subscribers.

Within a few weeks, we were turning over $1 million in revenue each week, and we were thrilled to be getting media attention. *Today Tonight* and *A Current Affair* ran segments about GroceryRun and how to buy cheap groceries online and we advertised in most publications in Australia.

The success achieved by Grocery Run made a big impact on the online world. It opened suppliers' eyes to new avenues for revenue outside of bricks and mortar and gave customers an exciting and convenient way to shop. But after 6 years of parallel growth, we decided that Catch should absorb Grocery Run and its customer base. This allowed customers the ability to buy their groceries as well as other products like footwear, beauty, fashion and pet products via Catchoftheday.

The Grocery Run ride is an experience that I'll never forget, and a legacy that I'm very proud to have been a part of and watch flourish.

Thanks to Kalman's initiative and persistence we became a real force in the grocery space. During the COVID-19 period of 2020, Catch dramatically increased its market share simply by letting its customer base know we were a source of hard-to-find products such as toilet paper, tinned goods, pasta, pharmaceuticals, cleaning products and more. A crisis such as COVID-19 will always present an opportunity for those who are awake and alert.

The success of Grocery Run made us ask, 'What other verticals could we move into?'

We'd accidentally stumbled on a winning formula of launching vertical businesses using the resources of what became known as the 'Catch Group' in that we had what many start-ups trying to enter the sector didn't. We had:

- a warehouse for receiving stock
- a healthy bank balance and cash flow
- a solid reputation (courtesy of the thousands of suppliers we'd done business with)
- a management team that was hungry to grow
- thousands of customers who trusted us.

Kalman Polak (front left) and the original Grocery Run team were always up for a (pyjama) party or two.

Mumgo. It's where mums go

The success of the niche site Grocery Run opened our eyes to new opportunities. We kept an eye on Baby Bunting and knew that the baby space was hot and could be a great area for us. It made sense. Our Catch customer base was 65 per cent women so it seemed obvious to launch a baby products site. The Catch website had become a valuable launch pad for testing other businesses—a perfect 'laboratory' where we could experiment with, and grow, new ideas and businesses—so we decided to use it to test the launch of this new site, and in July 2012 we launched Mumgo with a team of three people.

It started so well …

To build anticipation for the launch, and also to direct the right segment of our existing database to the new Mumgo site, we ran a competition to give away a Jeep (which they kindly gave us for free!). Within just a few weeks we had amassed huge interest, with more than 300 000 unique accounts registered before we even launched. To put this into perspective, it took Catchoftheday 18 months to reach 100 000 accounts.

The issues we had with attracting quality suppliers to Catch and then Grocery Run were not a problem for Mumgo. Unlike Catchoftheday, which was known for offering killer prices, Mumgo didn't look cheap or cut-price, which really helped brands such as Bonds, Heinz and Pampers (brands we'd coveted for years) to finally come on board.

Once Bonds came on board, other big brands such as Tommee Tippee and Playgro followed and when they started dealing with us (and liked us), they warmed to the idea of using Catchoftheday to list their products. Once the suppliers became aware of the vast volumes they could move on Catchoftheday, the question of supplying to us was never discussed again.

By the end of 2012, Mumgo had 20 staff, but while Mumgo was a fun addition to the group, it added a lot of supply chain complexities that created pressure for the team.

One unintended consequence of moving into the baby market was that we started to mess with the model of what made us so successful. Product selection is everything in the deal-buying world, and now we were selling something we'd never sold before—kids' and baby apparel—and, let us tell you, it's not easy for a stack of reasons. Clothes come in lots of sizes and colours and need to be handled with a lot more care than we were used to (as most of our products were housed in cardboard packaging), which slowed down the picking and packing process.

There were seasonality considerations too, and once a fashion trend had moved on, we often had leftover stock that we could never sell again. Add to this the complexities around the sorting, folding and storage of delicate garments, and you can see how quickly what was once a streamlined operation could blow out and cause bottlenecks throughout the entire warehouse operation. In addition, we also had to dedicate more space in the warehouse to storing this vast array of stock, and with space and dollars already constraining our growth, this new line of business only exacerbated our stress. In short, this supply chain was complex and complicated, it wasn't what we were used to and it was very disruptive.

Just as we 'decide by midnight and execute by midday' to start a business, the same applies when we stop a business, or in this case slow one down. So we made the hard call, and in 2013, only seven months in, scaled back the Mumgo business and refocused on our other core businesses. In theory, Mumgo was a great business concept, and if we hadn't been so busy, we could have given it the love and care it needed. But 2012 was a massive year of growth and expansion, and we just didn't have enough love to go around. We didn't completely shut it down. We kept it on simmer and at a size we could manage without it distracting the main business. Mumgo was operational until 2017 as a sub-site, offered a select range of deals already sold on Catchoftheday and provided mums with a one-stop-shop from which they could access the best brands at the best prices.

The reality for all entrepreneurs is that when you have 10 great ideas, nine of them will be the enemy of the best one.

Mumgo just had to go. Knowing when to keep going or sacrifice a business is critical to success. On this occasion, we had to put the brake on growth, and while it was painful for everyone concerned, it was the best decision for the business overall.

The launch of Vinomofo

VINOMOFO

Mumgo wasn't our only distraction that year. We made an investment in the high-end wine e-tailer Vinomofo, acquiring a 70 per cent stake in the Adelaide-based start-up run by three wine-preneurs: Andre Eikmeier, Justin Dry and Leigh Morgan. We loved the way they turned what we thought was a boring box of bottles into something sexy and we felt we could help them shift a lot of boxes.

The deal was done swiftly, and we were soon making waves as a serious player in the wine and spirit category. But despite our best efforts, it didn't work.

What went wrong? Three things:

1. Gabby, Hezi and Anees don't really drink, care about or understand wine and therefore couldn't tell the difference between a $5 bottle of wine and a $50 bottle of wine. And as such we couldn't really assist Vinomofo in growing the business because we just didn't understand their product.

2. The mofo founders (you can guess what that stands for) were fun guys to work with, but we seemed to have a difference in vision for Vinomofo. They preferred selling more high-end wines to wine-snobs at fair prices while we believed in the Dan Murphy style of 'stack-them-high-sell-them-at-killer-low-prices' school of retailing—the kind that appealed to a wider audience. You can see why this business relationship didn't work out in the end.

3. There was a lot going on in the business at that time. Even though we'd helped Vinomofo acquire several hundred thousand members and generate revenues of

$250 000+ per week, we found that it required quite a lot of management time and resources to keep it growing, and since our visions for the business weren't aligned with those of its founders, it made more sense to allocate more of that limited time and those resources to the business units that were strategically aligned.

So, it was no surprise when the founders approached us and asked to buy the business back.

The second deal was done just as fast as the first one. We were nice guys, they were nice guys; we just weren't meant to get married so quickly and we were both too young to realise it. So, in June 2013, exactly a year after joining us, the mofos departed with a business five times larger than what they arrived with, moved into a funky office in the hipster suburb of Richmond, Melbourne, and continued to successfully build the business. We'll drink to that!

You don't have to be tech savvy to launch a tech start-up

Neither of us are super tech savvy and we've never read or written a line of code. It takes many different types of skills to build a successful business, including a tech business, and you don't need to be a master of them all.

It may surprise you to discover that we're not finance experts either. Believe it or not, we've never ourselves created a profit and loss statement and would probably get a C grade for understanding a full one. However, that's also never been a problem.

Don't ever let your perceived limitations dictate your direction or future.

It takes a mix of people with different strengths to build a successful business.

The secret is to find out what you're good at and what you're passionate about, and then find a way to do more of that. You can hire or partner up with experts to take care of the important stuff you're not so good at.

Kissing frogs

The stories of Mumgo and Vinomofo can be viewed as stories of failure (or more specifically, a lack of focus), but failure is part of the entrepreneurial journey and it's the only way to learn. Being able to admit you made mistakes, and then being able to make fast decisions to stem the losses, is part and parcel of what being a successful entrepreneur is all about. To find entrepreneurial success, you've got to kiss a few frogs and hope one turns into a princess. We certainly had a few in our pond.

While we had enormous success with Catch, Grocery Run and Scoopon, and limited success with Mumgo and Vinomofo, we had no success with:

- *Yumtable:* a last-minute restaurant table reservation, table ordering and payment app (a great idea but ahead of its time)

> TO FIND ENTREPRENEURIAL SUCCESS, YOU'VE GOT TO KISS A FEW FROGS AND HOPE ONE TURNS INTO A PRINCESS.

- *Didgio:* a platform for buying and playing movies, video games and other software titles (another great idea killed by streaming players)

- *Atlas.com.au:* our first attempt at a marketplace, but it was too early for Australian retailers to understand and embrace.

Ever heard of any of these? We didn't think so. For one reason or another, mostly timing and resources, these ideas didn't fly. That's not to say we didn't try. We gave all these ideas 100 per cent of our energy and commitment. We spent millions trying to breathe life into them and hired talented teams to bring the concepts to fruition, but for a range of reasons, the ideas just didn't work. Simple as that.

And then came our Cinderella. The Fair-Etail continues …

It all started with pizza

EAT NOW

If we told you that we could launch a start-up in the uber-competitive field of food delivery, merge it with the market leader and sell the whole shebang to a global conglomerate less than three years later for $855 million, you'd tell us 'you're dreaming'.

But that's exactly what happened when we launched EatNow.

We still pinch ourselves sometimes and wonder how we managed to make it happen. It's a long story, but we'll just give you the highlights.

Hezi

The departure of Vinomofo and Mumgo created a vacuum, and there's nothing we like less than a vacuum (except the Dyson stick vac ones. We sold 3000 of them in one day, by the way).

When I look back on this era it feels like a crazy dream, but it was real and it all started with a pizza order.

'No pork,' I said to the pizza shop guy on the phone. Sure enough, the pizza arrived covered in ham. I was tired, pissed off and hungry. Not a good combination.

I rang the pizza guy back.

'I said no pork'.

He said, 'It's ham'.

'That is pork!'

This incident bugged me beyond belief. Administrative errors, ordering by phone, incorrect data entry: this kind of minutiae does my head in, and while they're tiny nuisances, the combination of all three made me think, 'there's got to be a better way to order food'.

I remembered a website I used once before to order my takeaway called Menulog. Although it seemed a little outdated, and even though most of my favourite restaurants weren't featured on there, the concept and process were actually quite useful. I started imagining building a slick app with all my favourite restaurants on it: a cool brand, a 'quick reorder' button for all my favourite restaurants and dishes ... I literally started salivating at the thought of what it could do and be.

As it happened, not long after the 'pork' incident, by real chance and perfect timing, I got a cold-call email from Matt Dyer (the most valuable cold call Matt ever made), a young Melbourne entrepreneur seeking help to scale a food app delivery business called EatNow.com.au.

Despite being in business for a few years, the website was only generating around one hundred orders a day. The orders were manually processed and actually faxed to the restaurants! Matt was only making a few hundred dollars a day in turnover and hardly enough to sustain or grow the business. It had a staff of three (Matt, his mum and his brother-in-law). There was no app and the look of the website even made Menulog's website look like a beauty queen. Having said that, it was functional. I placed an order, I got my food and I started to get really excited about what this little app could become.

Matt and I had coffee the next day and he was very impressive. He was a nice, humble guy who recognised his strengths and weaknesses. He was a good tech developer, knew the business and understood the fundamentals of the industry, but didn't have the knowledge in sales and marketing, expertise or experience in fast scale-ups, or funds to survive, let alone compete with Menulog.

It was everyone's lucky day.

Scoopon was in good hands under the leadership of Jon Beros, and the Catch businesses were scaling up big time in Braeside with Gabby, Anees and Kalman at the helm. It gave me the opportunity and time to again sink my teeth into a brand-new opportunity for the group.

After the coffee, I said to Matt I'd give him a call the next day. When Matt left, I crossed the road to a restaurant that had the Menulog service. It was the middle of the day and the owner wasn't busy. I started chit chatting and asked him what he liked and disliked about Menulog. I learned some great insights in 15 minutes that inspired me to take this on.

I called Matt the next day, we quickly agreed on terms and it wasn't long before we both moved into a newly rented office in Elsternwick (because both the Catch and Scoopon offices were bursting at the seams with staff). I finally managed to convince my friend Jason Rudy, who worked for a publicly listed, digital trading platform, to hang up his suit and give the start-up scene a shot as general manager. I hired a small team of sales people with whom I'd worked before and we brought on some developers. We spent six months building it up from scratch and in October 2012 we launched a brand-new website, platform and app.

One notable hire was Nathan Airy, a 21 year old from Queensland with a huge appetite for work and an even bigger appetite for success. He came to Melbourne for the interview, got the job that day, flew back to Queensland to pack up, and arrived back at the Melbourne office the next day, suitcase in hand, to start work. I was impressed.

'What about your girlfriend?' I asked. 'Is she coming?'

'I don't know,' he said. 'She doesn't know I've left. She's in Bali.'

His girlfriend eventually moved to Melbourne to be with him (and now they're married) but I mention this because it's this kind of commitment we loved seeing in our team.

The first mover advantage

The first one to take a product or service to market is known as the one who has the 'first mover advantage'. The first mover has an edge and can take time to develop their brand and set up expectations for future competition. Is it better to be first or second to market? It depends. For example, when we launched EatNow, we were seven years behind Menulog, so they had a distinct advantage in that they had an established brand, customers and loyalty.

But second movers can leverage the good and the bad of the first mover's road to success, and can also build on what the first mover has started. We had an advantage in that Menulog had spent a lot of years and money educating vendors about online ordering. No easy feat. Also, we could rectify some of the mistakes they were making that were too difficult or expensive for them to correct.

For example, the machines they used to send orders to restaurants were quite expensive to purchase and the software on them was owned by the hardware company, which charged an expensive licensing fee. Also, only that software company could make any changes to the software, so releasing any new features would have been difficult for Menulog. The high price of the machine and software was being charged back to the merchant to pay for the machine. We saw this as a weakness for Menulog and an opportunity for us. It wasn't easy, and it required hundreds of hours and an unbelievable effort, but we managed to not only source the hardware direct from the manufacturer overseas at a fraction of the price of the local seller, but also to write and therefore own the entire operating software for the ordering machines. We built them so cheaply, we were now able to offer merchants the hardware and software for free, while Menulog was charging them hundreds!

There are other benefits to being second or even third—for example, it's easier to determine whether there's a market from which you can take a slice. Many markets are fragmented and shared among thousands of brands, retailers and sites, both online and bricks and mortar. There is a lot of power in being the first to market, so be first if you can.

If you can't be first, be second—but let's be honest, in many segments of the market if you're not in the top three, you don't really exist.

Success was almost immediate

In less than a year EatNow went from 800 orders a week to 12 500 orders a week. From around thirty-thousand dollars a week in turnover to half a million dollars a week! We grew fast, won awards and started to frighten Menulog, the market leader.

Unfortunately, however, around the time we launched, so did Delivery Hero, one of the most cashed-up operators in the global sector. They certainly didn't make life easy for us when they started handing out millions in cash credits to entice customers to use their service. But the spirit of David against Goliath kicked in and the memory of Groupon trying to usurp Scoopon all those years ago emboldened us to believe that we could beat these suckers at their own game. Sometimes it's not the size of the dog in the fight but the size of the fight in the dog, and we were nothing if not hungry and pulling at the leash to take the lead on this one.

We certainly couldn't beat them with our small budget and tight resources so we knew we had to find their weakness and do what we do best: outsmart them, work harder and keep moving fast. While it was hard going, we just kept ploughing on and eventually they decided this yappy little dog was going to cause them too much grief, so they just packed up and went home.

> SOMETIMES IT'S NOT THE SIZE OF THE DOG IN THE FIGHT BUT THE SIZE OF THE FIGHT IN THE DOG.

One down. One to go.

Share ideas

If you swap an apple with a friend, you each have an apple. If you share an idea with a friend, you each have two ideas.

We've had many entrepreneurs tell us they have a 'great idea' for a business but that they can't tell us about it because they're scared that someone will grab the idea, become the next billionaire and leave them with nothing.

The days of keeping your wisdom and ideas close are over. Is there truly a unique idea anymore? Ideas are 'open source' concepts; how can you claim ownership over them?

On the flip side, we are proud to admit that all our businesses are either copied, replicated or inspired from one or a combination of other businesses mostly based outside of Australia. We took our inspiration from them, and built on those concepts to launch our own unique take on that business model for the local market. From there, we evolved and innovated to ensure we caused as much disruption to the market as possible.

Start-ups are launched to solve an existing problem. For 99 per cent of the problems out there, chances are a solution already exists, someone is working on it, and you simply need to be there to improve, develop and take it to the next level.

The best way to beat your competition is to make the thousands of decisions that are needed to be made every day, faster.

The speed and quality of the execution of a decision is the true differentiator that determines who will succeed and who will fail.

Remember, if you don't take action to make something happen, then an idea is just an idea.

Photo by Josh Robenstone

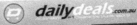

© Jesse Marlow / Fairfax Media

© David Geraghty / The Australian

© Paul Rovere / Fairfax Media

**Clockwise from top:
Hezi in our warehouse;
our first-ever team member
Vijay in our fully-automated
warehouse (2015); Gabby
and Hezi in the warehouse;
Gabby with a shopping trolley;
the amazing warehouse
team; our Moorabbin
warehouse (2010) [2];
Catch headquarters.**

Photo by Magnet-Me

© Aaron Francis / The Australian

© David Caird / The Australian

Where would you rather work: a fun place or a dud place?

The newspaper shown is the *Financial Review* with headlines:

US-Australia to secure rare earths

Tensions hit tourism from China

PC urges wages boost as RBA targets jobless

Caption under the photo: Catch Group founders Hezi and Gabby (seated) Leibovich, pictured in Paris, will pocket more than $200 million from the sale of Australia's oldest and largest online retailer to Wesfarmers.

Celebration was an important part of the Catch culture. When we sold to Wesfarmers, our celebrations even made it into the *Australian Financial Review*.

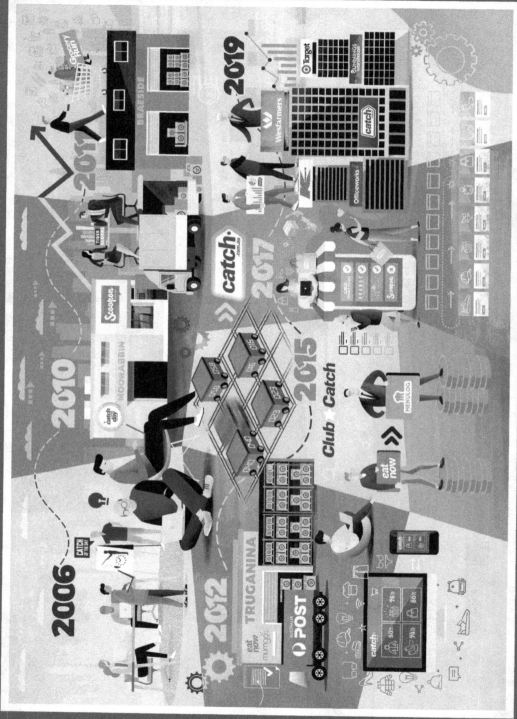

Designed by David Fajardo

Hezi

Meanwhile, the local leader Menulog was still thriving and while we were growing faster than them and grabbing some of the pie, we couldn't make any money. In fact, we were losing $200 000 every month! But we knew we had the right business model, the right tech and the right team and that with a bit more time we could scale, but we were definitely under pressure to find success fast.

In desperation to keep going, we decided to seek out investors to help fund our expansion. The underlying fundamentals were strong:

- 50 000 orders per month
- gross revenue of $2 million per month
- gross profit of $250 000 per month
- growth at 25 per cent per month.

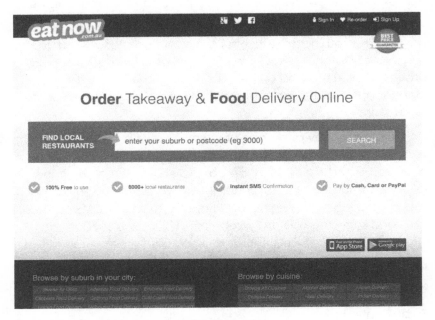

This is the original EatNow landing page.

We set up 10 meetings with high-net-worth individuals, wealthy families and venture capitalists (VCs) to see if they were interested in co-funding our growth.

The pitch was irresistible:

Give us $1 million in cash to run it for a year. In return, we value the business at (a very low) $5 million and you get 20 per cent equity.

The deal was a no-brainer, but everyone, and I mean everyone— even some of the smartest people I know—turned us down.

Where's the vision, people? In their eyes, it was too good to be true. Another misconception in business. Sometimes things aren't too good to be true. They're just good. This was one of them.

Menulog was still a serious thorn in our side, but with our customer-focused efforts we were making gains. So much so that Dan Katz, Menulog's CEO, rang me. He had rung me before, mainly to complain about some of his staff leaving to join EatNow. Still, the communication lines were open and we felt comfortable calling each other. Besides, while he was our direct competitor, I've always believed you need to keep your friends close but your enemies closer.

He said something to the effect of 'Congratulations on the success of Catchoftheday and Scoopon, but you guys should probably know that this online takeaway game is very different. Margins are tight, it's capital intensive and we've got a few years' head start.'

Dan is a lovely guy and none of it was said with arrogance. He was trying to tell us we were on a good wicket with the other businesses and that it may be best to stick to what we know. (It's not terrible advice in general but we actually thrived on exploring things we didn't know.) I did try to read between the lines and knew this couldn't just be a Dr Phil couch session.

My reply was,

'Thanks for the advice Dan, but how much are you offering?'

To be continued …

Doing the right thing

To say we had multiple irons in the fire at this time would be an understatement. We were trying to juggle several new businesses for the group, each growing fast but needing more focus and resources than we could sometimes give them. As every juggler knows, one distraction can make the whole thing tumble and crash. What came next wasn't just a distraction—it was like seeing a truck (or as it happens, a plane) about to fall on you while keeping all the balls in the air.

A serious matter at Scoopon Travel needed our urgent attention and called into question everything we as a group stood for.

Here's what happened.

Scoopon was firing on all cylinders (we'd just sold 675 000 Hungry Jacks vouchers within a few hours) and we'd just started getting traction in the travel sector.

As always, we were open to opportunities, so when Strategic Airlines came calling to offer us discounted airfares to exotic locations, we were interested. The deal was compelling. A return airfare to Phuket, Thailand, for around six-hundred dollars including meals, drinks and more! We were in.

Within 24 hours, we'd sold deals netting almost $1.2 million in revenue. We were so excited at how this deal had 'taken off', we ran another one, and this one sold out in less than 24 hours too. These were hot deals our customers loved!

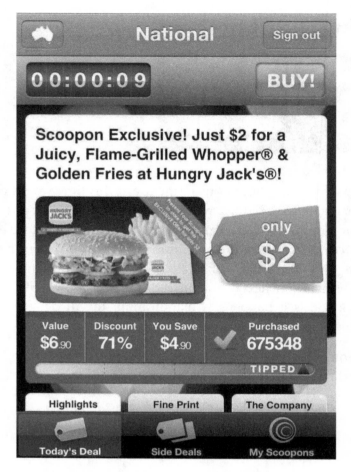

Scoopon sold 675 000 $2 meal deals from Hungry Jacks in a few hours.

A few weeks after the second deal went live, Strategic Airlines changed their name to Air Australia, to represent a stronger 'brand alignment' with Australian travellers. Or so they said. This branding-on-the-run activity raised alarm bells.

On 17 February 2012, the worst-case scenario happened. Air Australia went bankrupt and they couldn't even pay for the fuel to get their planes from Phuket back to Australia. No amount of due diligence on our behalf could have foreseen this event occurring. It was a once-in-a-million risk and yet it happened, and we had to deal with it. We scrambled to comprehend the complexities of what it meant to us and more importantly, to our customers.

As you can imagine, our travellers, who were either in the middle of their holiday or planning one, panicked, wondering if their deal would be honoured (or even if they could get home to Australia!). Technically speaking, we weren't obliged to honour the deal as we had already paid Air Australia for the tickets; we were not holding the customers' money and the obligation to refund their fares sat well and truly with Air Australia, or their insurance company.

But of course, the traveller, who bought the deal from Scoopon, could be forgiven for thinking that Scoopon should honour the deal. We'd sold 4000 deals and 2000 of them had yet to redeem their deal so we were looking down the barrel of refunding $1 million in airfares for a disaster that we had no hand in creating. We had to make a decision, and it's times like this the core values of a company come into play.

We had two options: cut the travellers loose and let them try their luck with getting their money back from Air Australia. Or, refund the customers, take a hit of $1 million and help expatriate them back to Australia as quickly as we could.

We chose the latter. Even though it wasn't, technically speaking, our problem to solve, we made it our problem to solve. Our DNA has always been 'customer first' and this was no different. Financially speaking, it was a tough decision to make. Morally and ethically, it was an easy decision to make. We felt obliged to ensure none of our customers were left stranded.

Once the commitment to help our customers had been made, we immediately set up a taskforce to deal with the situation. We boosted our customer service team to work around the clock to take any calls from customers; sent Scoopon representatives to Phuket airport to help our customers; booked them on alternative flights; and offered them free accommodation if a flight was not available. It's worth noting, we believe we were the first travel company to offer our customers full refunds—and this from a two-year-old start-up—while other travel companies (worth billions) chose not to.

Doing the right thing is easy when it doesn't cost you.

But when the price tag is $1 million (or $2 million really, as we'd already paid Air Australia $1 million for the airfares, and were now refunding the customers another $1 million out of our own pocket) and you're bootstrapping a fledgling start-up, doing the right thing can become a very painful and expensive exercise.

But as we discovered, sometimes doing the right thing isn't just good for the customer, it can be good for the company too. This experience taught us a lot about what it means to honour your values. By doing so, we built trust with our travel customers, which took our relationship with them to a whole new level.

Although unintended, this action to refund our customer base, which received unprecedented media coverage, elevated us from a little-known entity in the air travel sector to becoming a household name for buying travel. What could have been our biggest setback became our greatest asset. This incident signalled to our customers and suppliers that even if the shit hits the fan and the deal falls over, we will do the right thing by them. Trust. It's a valuable currency that we take seriously and it's another reason why we've been able to weather the retail storms for so long while other, larger, more established brands have fallen by the wayside.

Scoopon ended up growing throughout the rest of the year and finished FY2012 with revenues of $80 million, which wasn't bad for a two-year-old business.

CHAPTER 9

The robots are coming!

Once we had this travel matter under control, we as a management team had to face another expensive issue that had been bothering us for a long time. It was a situation we could no longer ignore. The problem? We were just growing too fast and our warehousing facility could not keep up.

Logistics is not a sexy topic to most, but it is to us because it's the beating heart behind the success of our business. Stick with us as we tell you why, because the story of how we came to revolutionise our logistics system and install one of the world's most advanced robotic warehouse systems encapsulates the essence of what made us so successful as a business.

For a start, what does logistics even mean? To us, it's 'how do we pack lots of items into a box and ship them to our customers quickly, while still turning a profit at the end of the month?' We had almost 40 000 m² of warehouse space spread over two locations, with 200 staff, so to automate something of this scale was seriously challenging.

Vijay was part of the team tasked with finding a new solution.

Vijay

Both warehouses were completely manual, meaning everything was done the good-old way: by team members walking, pushing, counting, sorting, picking and packing everything by hand.

As a result, each order took us 10 minutes to pack and each picker walked at least 10 kilometres a day to source the stock and pack it up.

While everything was manual and the system worked well when we were doing a single deal per day, it didn't work when we suddenly found ourselves with a range of 7000 different SKUs (stock-keeping units) in the warehouse.

We looked around to see if anyone else was doing anything remotely like this but the search was fruitless. There was not one business in Australia at that time dealing with the volume and operational complexity we were facing.

The downside of being market leaders in e-commerce in Australia was that we were regularly faced with lots of unique challenges that no-one else was experiencing yet.

The solution? We took a leaf out of our Mazal playbook and went out to educate ourselves: Gabby, Vijay and Tim, our chief operations officer, spent months touring some impressive local warehouses and talking to the top experts in the business about a possible solution. We even popped over to Singapore to inspect a bunch of newly launched robotic systems.

As the search for a warehouse solution progressed, the business kept growing so we had to scale up on the run. For example, at the start of our search, we had a budget of $3 million to spend on a warehouse solution that could handle 5000 products. Three months later, the volume of products we had to manage had grown to 10 000. Three months later, 15 000. Did we mention growing pains?

Within six months of setting out on our educational journey, we'd made a decision. We decided to implement an Autostore robotic warehouse system, which would enable us to fully automate our picking and packing process.

Autostore is a six-metre-high Rubik's cube–style box containing 25 000 plastic bins, each the size of a large microwave, stacked on top of each other. The cube is covered with a massive grid and 70 bright red robots shuttle across the top of the grid to dip down and retrieve the bins as needed and then shuffle each bin filled with the right stock to the 'pick and pack' stations on the ground below. Think of it as a gigantic game of Tetris*.

So, 12 months and an investment of $20 million later, we became the proud owners of one of the smartest, fastest and most space-saving automated warehouse systems available, and the first distribution centre in Australia to have one. The benefits of the system were numerous. We could increase our range and our speed of packing/shipping, and reduce the error rate as well, all of which helped us maintain our commitment to offering the highest standards of customer service.

The best part about our new robots? They didn't take the weekend off, have smoko breaks or get tired. Automation heaven.

The very best bit? We didn't lay off a single worker throughout the entire automation change-over. In fact, the introduction of the system actually generated *more* employment opportunities because we were now able to promote more products and ship them more quickly. We were very pleased with and proud of this achievement.

---

* Search 'Autostore—Catchoftheday' on YouTube and watch the videos. It's phenomenal to see it in action. The video is also on catchofthedecade.com.

Our warehouse prior to automation.

As part of this growth phase, we employed an exceptional warehouse manager by the name of Saar Davidi. He joined us soon after the automation process began to bring everything back in order.

Saar

While the search took longer than we thought, cost more than we thought and was harder to implement than we thought, it paid off. Being first to market with this system put us ahead of our competitors in leaps and bounds and allowed us to fast track our growth in the years to come.

Our warehouse after automation. It cost us $20 million to build, but it set us up for the future.

The one major stuff-up we made in this whole automation journey was in our timing. We made the silly mistake of trying to integrate the automation process into the warehouse in the months of October and November (2014). We had two choices to make. If we could get the automation done on time, we would be able to fulfil the large anticipated Christmas trade order volumes.

Without a new warehouse system, we probably couldn't. However, if we weren't able to get it done on time, we would be stuck with a partially functioning warehouse that would certainly not be able to fulfil the orders. Optimistically, we went for it and we failed. For all of you online retailers out there thinking of doing something similar just before the busiest time of the year, please don't! As any retailer will know, the third quarter of the year is 'the money quarter' where you make 40 to 70 per cent of your yearly profits. Sadly, because of this timing decision, we made no profit in the last three months of that year. All of our profits were spent on extra staff and integration costs within our warehouse. For a retailer counting on the Christmas sale period this was a massive letdown.

Today, Saar manages Catch's operation from a distribution centre at Truganina, Victoria, and has built one of the best performing hubs in the country. This well-oiled operation is one of the main factors that attracted Wesfarmers to team up with us (more on that later).

Saar is much more than a warehouse manager. He lives and breathes the Catch DNA. He is an intrapreneur of the highest order, an employee who behaves as if he owns the business. He drove 90 minutes each way to get to work and home, but he was always the last one to stay back and fix that thing that needed doing. We'll never forget the time the warehouse roof sprung a massive leak. He could have called a tradesperson to fix it, but that would have taken a day or more. Instead, he found a ladder, gathered up the required tools, crawled into the roof cavity and fixed it himself, there and then. He didn't have to do it; it wasn't his job, but he knew it would save us a headache. That's the kind of attitude that makes him, and people like him, so indispensable to Catch.

Spot the intrapreneurs within your company and let them get on with it

Intrapreneurship: the act of behaving like an entrepreneur while working within a large organisation

Intrapreneurs are employees inside a company who act like entrepreneurs. They may not own the business, but they commit to it as if it were theirs. We've had a lot of people like that at Catch over the years. They're the caring, hard-working, proactive, creative leaders who take on any responsibility and run with it. They develop original ideas. They invent new solutions. They act intelligently and decisively. They are team players, authentic, likeable, sincere and always there when they're needed.

In management circles, these people are known as intrapreneurs. In our world, they're known as the ones with the 'Catch DNA'.

Everyone who works with them knows they're the real deal. Think about it. It probably won't take you two seconds to name the intrapreneurs in your organisation. Over the years, our Catch intrapreneurs (and we've had dozens of them!) have pushed our businesses forward. Many of them are named in this book, and there are many more we didn't have room to name. Names that come instantly to mind include Kalman Polak and Guy Polak. They were the first to arrive, last to leave, worked around the clock when needed, held the Catch DNA flame alight when we were there and kept it alight when we left. Intrapreneurs like them are the secret sauce, the rocket fuel, the steroids that bulk up your business, and if you haven't yet identified them, you should. And when you do, empower them to get on with it, and then get out of their way, because the results they'll deliver are in direct proportion to the freedom you give them.

We believe that today Guy and Kalman are Australia's best e-commerce minds, having learned the trade at the University of Catch.

Gabby

I remember walking through the warehouse one day when a young staff member of the packing team approached me.

'Hi,' he said. 'My name is Soji and I would love to have some of your time to chat with you about my observations on the packing floor'.

The other 99 packers must have thought Soji was mad, or out of line, to stop the owner and bother him with his ideas and suggestions. I didn't think he was mad. I appreciated his bravery in speaking up.

Soji was one of 100 packers walking kilometres every day to pack an order, and thanks to his willingness to 'step out of line' his ideas went on to help us implement a range of changes that dramatically improved our receiving and dispatch functions. It's this kind of 'big head' thinking we looked for, and encouraged in our team. Soji's bravery was rewarded. He is now the head of our receiving department, is one of the five top leaders at Australia's best distribution centre, and I am also honoured to call him my friend.

Hezi

Another colleague who demonstrated this 'big head' mentality was Nati Harpaz. Prior to hiring him to be our CEO in 2016, we'd bumped into him at various industry events and conferences, and one thing that always caught our eye was he was never too shy to raise his hand in a room full of people to ask the speaker a challenging question. That quality endeared him to us and was a key reason we appointed him to run the business. More on that later.

The lesson?

If you can't solve a problem, it's because you are playing by the rules,

so step out of the straight jacket and encourage your team to demonstrate big head thinking. You may find it cracks the problem wide open.

Step out of line

To be a disruptor, you have to occasionally break the rules and challenge conventional thinking. This takes courage and guts. Most people are too shy or scared to do that so they go with the flow and great ideas get missed, or worse, stupid ideas get endorsed. In Hebrew, we call it *rosh katan*, a term that everyone understands. In English, it's called 'small head mentality':

I will come to work every day, do what I am told, not upset anyone and have an easy life.

And then there's *rosh gadol*. That's Hebrew for 'big head mentality':

I will always step out of line and challenge the status quo. If I spot something that is not done correctly, I will alert my team members and we will fix the problem.

When hiring we always looked for big heads and avoided small heads. It paid off.

Celebrating the Indian holiday of Onam. L to R: Saar, Vijay2, Gabby, Soji, Hezi and Ryan Gracie.

CHAPTER 10
The Catch culture

We've never understood why employees who leave the corporate sector to set up their own business often drag with them the exact culture they were trying to escape. Why would you take so much risk and invest so much time and energy only to recreate the same bullshit atmosphere that you hated in the first place? Most of us spend more than one-third of our lives at work (maybe more!) so it makes sense to create a workplace culture that excites you and your team.

By mid 2013, it was obvious that we were successful in creating a place where people wanted to work—maybe too successful, as we now had 400 people crammed into three sites around the suburbs of Melbourne. To say this wasn't ideal was an understatement, and the problem wasn't going to go away. We were still hiring like crazy and we had nowhere for them to sit! The workplaces were bursting at the seams.

The fact our office and warehouse locations were not located in the hipster suburbs of Richmond and South Melbourne—where the millennial technerati prefer to work from—said volumes about

> IT WAS OBVIOUS THAT WE WERE SUCCESSFUL IN CREATING A PLACE WHERE PEOPLE WANTED TO WORK—MAYBE TOO SUCCESSFUL

our culture. Despite our daggy suburban locations, we attracted the best and the brightest from around the country and they didn't mind working far from the epicentres of disruption because they loved working for us. So, as we looked for a new home for all of our businesses under one roof, we were fortunate that we didn't feel the need to move to one of those expensive innovation hubs. We could go where we had space to grow.

Sliding into greatness

We toured the recently vacated former headquarters of Adidas Australia in the south-eastern suburb of Mulgrave. While the rent was three times more than what we'd ever paid, it was love at first sight. The massive 5000 m² space was spread over two floors and had plenty of room for all of our businesses. Adidas was kind enough to leave us a working gym and, outside, a basketball court and beautiful garden. Good luck finding that in the CBD.

All the furniture was still intact, too, from the deck chairs to the boardroom conference table. All we had to do was walk in, plug in and start working. And Adidas left behind one more thing that really sealed the deal, the slogan that greeted everyone at the door: 'Impossible is Nothing'.

It still seems impossible that we agreed to management's request to spend more than one million dollars in rent per year for that space, but what can we say? We were on a high. We felt invincible at that stage on our journey. Nothing seemed impossible. It didn't stop there. We ended up installing a slide so staff members could slide from the upper floor to the ground floor. Now, we admit, not many people took the slide. It was a bumpy, twisty ride, and God help you if you tried it with a cup of coffee in your hand. But every person who walked in the door, whether it was a new supplier or a prospective employee or the postman, must have told their friends about this crazy office with a slide because it was the first thing people wanted to see when they visited the building.

Our Mulgrave headquarters quickly became notorious in the start-up community. The new building was also a major drawcard for our HR department. Talented people who had never even heard of Mulgrave before would come for an interview, have their heads turned by the atmosphere, and be on staff and in the thick of things before they knew what had happened. Most importantly, every reporter who ever stopped by included the slide in their story. It paid for itself in free PR alone.

Interestingly, our office on Springvale Rd, Mulgrave, was exactly opposite the head office of Kmart Australia. We watched them every day, and we are certain that they looked at us. Quite often many of us would cross the road to eat lunch and grab a coffee from the Kmart cafeteria, which was open to the many offices in the area. Who would have known that five years later our companies would merge?

Why not make it fun?

Where would you rather work: a fun place or a dud place? How would you rather your employees feel in the morning: psyched up and excited about getting to work, or dreading it and dreaming of all the places they'd rather be? How would you rather your employees feel in the evening: happy to stay a bit longer to get the job done, or watching the clock until it hits 5 pm and rushing out the door?

Who would you rather hire: someone who could get a job anywhere but really wants to be part of your team, or someone with no other prospects because the top talent all went somewhere else?

The answers are obvious. So, it's obvious why you should invest some time into making your office a fun place to be.

Fortunately, it doesn't have to be expensive. Not everyone can have a gym or a slide in their head office, but you don't need them to create a fun, friendly workplace. It's amazing how far a Friday barbecue or a dress-up day can go in breaking down barriers, loosening people up and making friendships.

If people have friends at work, they'll be excited to come to the office.

It felt good for us to see 10 IT guys taking a walk every afternoon, the customer service teams playing basketball and the buyers having massive birthday lunches. That's how we knew our teams were strong: they spent time together when they didn't have to.

Besides, it's not just better for your staff to have fun at work. It's better for you. You'll spend most of your time at work. Make sure it's fun.

REMEMBER, YOU'RE AN ENTREPRENEUR, SO YOU MAKE THE RULES. DON'T SENTENCE YOURSELF TO ANOTHER SHITTY JOB.

Negotiating in pyjamas

This fun spirit can have a powerful impact on your brand in other ways, too. One day, we had senior executives from Australia Post coming in to discuss a major deal. We were spending eight figures with them, so it was an important meeting.

It just so happened that we had a staff dress-up day scheduled, where everyone—management included—committed to showing up in pyjamas, irrespective of what meetings we had on or who was visiting. The Australia Post executives were sitting on one side of the boardroom in their three-piece suits and shiny shoes, when in we walked, clad in our Bob the Builder and Dora the Explorer sleepwear.

For a start, the looks on their faces were priceless. But second, it broke the ice and created lots of laughs before we got down to the serious business of negotiating pricing.

Our in-house café was the heart of Catch. It's where parties, celebrations and all major announcements took place.

Events like this create an impression that doing business with Catch is a positive experience. They go back to their office saying,

'How crazy are those Catch guys? We just had a meeting and they were all dressed in pyjamas! They're insane!'

If 'brand' is what people say about you when you're out of the room, we were pretty sure people were saying Catch looked like a fun place to work. Our reputation for creating a happy workplace created a powerful word-of-mouth effect that made hiring new employees a piece of cake. (Which, by the way, we ate a lot of at Catch. Never let a birthday go to waste!)

We rarely advertised because as soon as we had an opening, our staff would put the word out to their personal networks and do the recruitment for us. Later on, we did spend more than $600 000 one year on recruitment fees to hire new staff, so take it from us: it's much cheaper and faster to hire from internal recommendations. And the results are just as good, maybe better, because your culture is your people.

Your culture is your people

Our philosophy has always been, 'hire for attitude, train for skill'. You can teach skills. You can't teach attitude. After hiring more than 2000 people, we know a thing or two about who makes a great team player and who doesn't.

Someone who's curious, energetic, involved, puts the team first and always looks for a way to get things done: these people would always find a place at Catch. Get enough of them together, working every day for the same goal, and you create a company that can do anything. You get a happy company and happy people.

Gabby and Hezi in the office celebrating a team member's birthday. Never let a good birthday go to waste!

Happy people are more effective, happy people create solutions, happy people share ideas and speak up, happy people engage in change and allow for innovation to take place.

It has to be said: we had a happy workplace!

On the other hand, get enough people together who are lazy, or self-centred, or toxic (more on that later), and it doesn't matter what big companies are on their résumé, or how many programming languages they know: no amount of training can alter their attitude. They'll take the company down with them.

Be a mensch

Of course, as leaders we have to set the example. If you're the boss, be a *mensch*. That's Yiddish for a nice guy. If leaders behave with integrity and respect, their teams will do the same. If leaders behave poorly, then it sets the standards for everyone else to behave poorly. Some say 'nice guys finish last', but we don't agree. It's no fun being nasty. We much prefer the carrot to the stick, and besides, the 'don't be a jerk' approach yields better results.

As an entrepreneur, being a mensch also means giving as much, or more, to the company as you ask of your employees. If you're not doing your part, your staff will notice and adjust their own efforts accordingly. Can you blame them? For example, if you need your employees to stay late, you can't clock off in time to go home and watch the 6 pm news. If that's what you want out of life, working in a start-up is probably not for you.

If you need honest advice (and you do), you can't get angry when people tell you some truths you don't want to hear, or ask inconvenient questions. Everyone should be encouraged to challenge everyone else, or your business will suffer from small head mentality. If you can't handle challenges from within your team, you're not ready to handle the challenges from your competitors.

If you need people to watch your back, you have to watch theirs. A little kindness and flexibility can work wonders in helping you build a loyal family around you. The truth is, you will probably spend more time with these people than with your own family. Loyalty is a two-way street.

And you have to be the first to get stuck in. We were always at work, always ready to be involved in any decision, always putting our own opinions on the line. Culture is what happens when the leader isn't looking. The more staff members see their leaders doing the right thing, working as hard as anyone, the sooner they will understand what the company needs and follow that lead, even when the boss is on holiday.

Ready for something mind-blowing? Being nice extends to your competitors, too. Even when it seems counter-intuitive to be nice, it's the right thing to do, and believe it or not, it pays off. When launching our new state-of-the-art warehouse, we invited 200 of our A-grade suppliers, and even the CEOs of competitive companies, to take a tour and see our amazing robots in action. Our automation process was the talk of the town and everyone wanted to see what we were doing. We were very open to sharing our trade secrets with our competitors. Everyone asked, 'Why would you do that?'

> **READY FOR SOMETHING MIND-BLOWING? BEING NICE EXTENDS TO YOUR COMPETITORS, TOO.**

We saw it as our responsibility to help educate the industry overall, and to create a sense of goodwill and camaraderie with everyone in the sector. Besides, it took us three years to build this warehouse, so if anyone wanted to go and 'copy' us, then so be it; it would take them three years to do the same.

And here's the kicker: a week later, five of those A-grade visitors signed up their premium brands to become Catch suppliers. We call that the karmic reaction. Make no mistake: if you're a jerk, word will travel fast and no-one will want to work with you, or for your business. If you're a mensch, word will also get around, and you'll have everyone lining up to work with you. Why not take the latter route? Not only is it good for business, but you get to sleep well at night too.

AIRheads need not apply

AIR stands for 'Arsehole In the Room'. You know the type: always dismissive of other opinions, making decisions that put their needs first, trying to stand out by bullying and putting others down. The AIRhead always takes credit for positive results, and never takes responsibility for negative ones.

Diagnosing the condition is difficult because the carriers are often very smart and good at their job. Their co-workers may consider them indispensable. This gives the arseholes more power and freedom to be even more destructive. Other employees see this behaviour being not just tolerated, but rewarded. The company descends into a toxic cesspool of chaos and conflict that can be difficult, if not impossible, to pull out of.

We've encountered AIRheads in every department, but mostly in the C-suite. You can move them around, you can read them the riot act, but it will be about as useful as moving the deck chairs on the *Titanic*. If someone on your team is displaying these symptoms, get rid of them. Permanently. Quickly. Today. Or your best team players will find somewhere less toxic to work, and you'll be left with nothing but AIRheads.

Shoot for the stars

Our favourite TV show was *Seinfeld*. Everyone on the team loved the show, especially Kalman Polak, who sometimes thought he was actually George Costanza. When Lee Fixel from Tiger asked us years earlier who our ideal 'brand ambassador' might be we instantly answered 'George' because he's a cheapskate and loves a bargain and everyone agreed he'd be our ideal 'Catch man'. We all laughed and promptly forgot about the conversation.

Years later, we saw that George (aka Jason Alexander) was performing at Crown Towers in Melbourne so we got in touch with his manager to see if he'd be interested in shooting a TV commercial for us. When he said 'yes', we were super excited to be meeting him in person.

He came over to the office, met the team, did the TV shoot as well as lots of still images, delivered us a private comedy show for family, friends, staff and suppliers and was super accommodating on so many levels.

For the next 12 months the 'George' advertising campaign was plastered all over our website, on trams, buses, trains and automobiles (no planes ...).

This spontaneous marketing campaign was incredibly successful, and not only established the Catchoftheday brand as a fun brand but also provided the entire team with some happy and unforgettable memories.

Who'd have thought a little start-up could secure a Hollywood star and legendary comic to be the face of its company? It just goes to show: if you aim for the stars and you hit the moon, you'll still come out ahead.

Kalman Polak (Head of Buying); Jason Alexander, aka George from *Seinfeld*, our Catch ambassador; and Guy Polak (Grocery Run). Yes, Kalman and Guy are brothers, in case you were wondering.

CHAPTER 11

Meanwhile, back at Menulog...

Meanwhile, Hezi and the EatNow team were growing the business aggressively, but at the same time, there was continual pressure to reduce the cash burn. Despite the amazing results, not everyone in management could stomach it.

It wasn't long before Dan Katz from Menulog called again and made us an offer to buy us out. How much? Ten million dollars. Not to be sneezed at, but we had other plans.

 Hezi

At this point, EatNow was still going through a hair-raising $200000 per month and while it was flying like a rocket and I was very confident, the mounting pressure from head office was starting to get to me. I seriously considered taking the $10 million.

In fairness, the pressure didn't come from a bad place. Burning cash regardless of growth was a very foreign concept in the group's management mentality, and we were also co-funding a number of other start-ups being built in-house, including Yumtable, Game, Didgio and Atlas, all of which weren't cheap to incubate and weren't bringing in any revenues yet. Some had not even been launched yet. At this point, we were spending a total of $600 000 a month on speculative businesses (which may or may not have made it) and the resultant pressure on all of us was intense. If we took this deal, it would enable us to not only stem our cash burn, but we would also recoup our losses and even make a tiny profit.

However, I had one word for Dan:

'No'.

I gave him a counter-offer: $12.5 million.

He had one word for me:

'No'.

In that moment, to be honest, I was so relieved. I knew it was the right decision to continue, and I was so glad the die had been cast by the other side and a sale was no longer an option.

With the distraction of a potential sale out of the way, we went back to the drawing board, worked our butts off, grew even faster, captured more market share and 12 months later, got another call from Dan.

'We're both knocking ourselves out, and losing a lot of money in the process trying to compete,' he said. 'Why don't we merge, list or sell the businesses together? After all, we are worth so much more together than separately.'

That call was music to my ears because our other Catch motto (we had a few of them) was that 'the sum of both parts is greater than the whole', and this truism certainly kicked in here. We negotiated a very fair 30/70 split (their way), the companies merged to become Menulog and we started our newly married life together with enthusiasm.

We engaged Goldman Sachs to manage the trade sale process. Combined, we were a clear market leader in the food delivery app market and that naturally commanded a premium from any buyer or investor.

The combined Menulog group was a very attractive proposition to many potential acquirers, both local and global, who saw it as a strategic opportunity. It was of interest to others who were simply financial types who loved the metrics and, in particular, the growth and market position of the combined business. It seemed like everyone wanted a slice of the expanding Australian food ordering market.

In June 2015, a mere 18 months after the launch of EatNow and only four months after we merged the Menulog and EatNow businesses, we took our seats at the Goldman Sachs boardroom in Melbourne. Surrounded by stakeholders who had been through an exhilarating rollercoaster from both EatNow and Menulog, we watched Dan take to the stage to announce that we had been sold to a large, publicly listed UK food ordering business called Just Eat.

Dan loves a bit of theatre. As the process was extremely confidential and 95 per cent of the people in the room were not privy to any of the bids or final sell price, Dan asked everyone to write down on a piece of paper what they thought we'd been bought for.

Most people wrote down somewhere between $150 million and $200 million.

A few others wrote down $250 million, or even $350 million.

Gabby, ever the optimist, wrote down $480 million.

The real figure we were sold for?

$855 million.

The room erupted into screams of delight. No-one, not even our closest friends, expected anything like this result.

I looked around at the beaming faces.

I will never forget the expression on Matt Dyer's face, the young founder who had come to me three years earlier, desperate to keep this fledgling idea alive when he was moments away from shutting it down. That look was priceless.

Actually, for many around the table this result did have a price. Matt, Nathan Airy and Jason Rudy, and many others around that room, became instant millionaires. It was less than two years earlier that I had described my vision to Matt, who was about to close his business down; Nathan, who was a 20-year-old kid on the Sunshine Coast with stars in his eyes; and Jason, who took a big leap of faith risking a cushy, high-paying corporate job to join us. I was so proud that despite all the odds, we delivered what we had promised one another. Together, we were unbeatable.

1 + 1 = 3 was at work.

1 (EatNow) + 1 (Menulog) = undisputed market leader.

P.S. Timing is everything in business. At the time of the sale, Uber Eats and Deliveroo did not exist in Australia. A year later and the result we achieved would have looked very, very different. Mazal was on our side again.

P.P.S. We train 'em well at Catch. Our motto of training leaders to become leaders showed up. We're proud to note that both of the current CEOs of Uber Eats and Deliveroo are former employees of Catch.

P.P.P.S. If those high net worth individuals had taken up the pitch offer, the $1 million they would have invested would have returned more than $50 million. As Julia Roberts said in *Pretty Woman*, 'Big mistake'.

A week before the announcement of the EatNow deal, the story was leaked to the media with a rumour it would sell for $500 million. The editor of *BRW* scoffed and said in a news story, 'If the merged companies sell for $500 million I'll eat my hat'. He's still munching. We had the last laugh on that one.

After just 18 months in business, we sold EatNow/Menulog for nearly one billion dollars: Nathan Airy, Gabby, Matt Dyer, Hezi and Jason Rudy after the announcement at the Goldman Sachs office.

The sum of the whole is bigger than the parts

<u>Much of our success comes down to our belief in the '1 + 1 = 3' principle.</u>

It underpins almost everything we do. It means that the sum of the whole is bigger than the parts. In other words, we are stronger if we collaborate than if we do it on our own. Gabby + Hezi together are a stronger team than just Gabby or Hezi on their own. Gabby/Hezi + Nati are a much stronger team than the three individuals working apart.

The principle doesn't just relate to collaborations between people, it applies to collaborations between businesses too.

1	+ 1	= 3
Catch	+ Kmart	= success
Menulog	+ EatNow	= $855 million and 95 per cent of the market
Bon Voyage	+ Scoopon Travel	= Luxury Escapes
Scoopon	+ Bon Voyage + Luxury Escapes	= massive business!

In conversations, we frequently used the term '1 + 1 = 3' when we felt really bullish about something. If we were really excited about something, we might even say '1 + 1 = 5'.

Having said that, mixing two or more things together doesn't always produce a great result. In fact, sometimes if you try to mix two things that are great individually but that don't complement or add value to each other, this can actually result in 1 + 1 = 0, or loss of value. Try cooking tuna and lamb together and you'll know what we mean.

When we contemplated mergers, our shareholders would often struggle to see how 1 + 1 = 3 worked. They would worry that as soon as the ink dried on that contract, they would own a smaller share of the deal—in other words that their ownership would go from 10 per cent to 5 per cent—arguing that the deal had now lost half its value. That's not how we saw it.

Take the EatNow merger as an example. For every day we operated, we wasted a lot of time and money defending ourselves from Menulog. We knew we could catch them, but it would take us two years and, in that time, we were at risk (as they were too) of being decimated if a global player such as Zomato, Deliveroo or Uber Eats arrived in the market.

In the back of our minds we knew that if Menulog and EatNow merged, it would be a marriage made in heaven. A merger would mean we would go from owning close to 100 per cent of EatNow, to owning less than one-third of the combined group, but it would be a smaller share of a much, much bigger pizza.

When we did merge in 2015, the business had a combined larger number of orders, revenue and customers, and through the consolidation of assets, we were also able to make the business more cost efficient as we now didn't need two separate offices in each city, two ordering systems, two marketing teams and the like. Up until this point it was a simple case of 1 + 1 = 2.

Source: Photo by Josh Robenstone

But the magic of 1 + 1 = 3 kicked in when we realised that the merger made us the undisputed number-one food ordering platform in Australia. Not only did this merger make it better for our customers (more restaurants to choose from) and our restaurants (more customers for them to market to), but it also meant that we could now defend ourselves against bigger threats, and importantly, become an attractive acquisition for a global company interested in entering the Australian market. And that's exactly what happened in 2015 when UK giant Just Eat swooped in and acquired us for $855 million, a figure that was far, far greater than the total value of Menulog and EatNow individually.

There is an additional lesson in all of this. Regardless of how fiercely you compete, always remember to create and maintain a communication channel with your competitors. It's very possible that you may one day be on the same team as your greatest rival, celebrating side by side.

Our deals attracted a lot of media attention, which generated even more media attention. 1 + 1 + 3.
Source: © Dynamic Business

Catches

1   Venture capital comes with extra pressure. Be prepared for scrutiny.

2   Growth is great, but it creates problems. You may need to pivot.

3   Product selection is everything. Sell what you know and understand.

4   If you need to shut down a business, do it quickly.

5   Knowing when to keep or kill an idea is critical to success.

6   If you have 10 great ideas, nine of them will be the enemy of the best one.

7   New ventures need love and care. Be sure someone is around to provide it.

8   You don't need to be tech savvy to launch a tech start-up. Find out what you are good at and do more of that. Hire experts to take care of everything else.

9   You need to kiss a few frogs to find your princess.

10 Failing is part of the entrepreneurial journey. It's the only way to learn.

11 If you make a mistake, act on it quickly, stem the losses and keep moving forward.

12 Not every idea succeeds.

13 Be open to hearing start-up pitches. It could be the next Afterpay.

14	Keep your friends close but your enemies closer. Your competitor could be your next collaborator.
15	Create and maintain a communication channel with your competitors. You may one day be on the same side.
16	When the shit hits the fan and your customers are impacted, do the right thing by them.
17	Time your innovations or new initiatives so they don't interfere with your major sales peaks.
18	Have a 'big head' mentality. Step out of line, challenge conventional thinking and have the courage to speak up.
19	If you can't solve a problem, it's because you are playing by the rules.
20	Create a workplace culture that excites you and your team.
21	A great culture will attract the best and the brightest talent, no matter where your office is located.
22	Make work fun. People will stay longer.
23	It doesn't cost a lot to create a fun workplace culture.
24	If you're the boss, you make the rules. Don't sentence yourself to another shitty job.
25	The show must go on(line). Digital is the future. Get used to it.
26	Happy staff will do your recruitment for you.
27	Hire for attitude, train for skill. You can teach skills. You can't teach attitude.
28	Be a *mensch*. That's Yiddish for a nice guy.
29	When leaders behave with integrity and respect, the teams will do the same.
30	Nice guys don't finish last.

31 Being nice extends to your competitors, too. It's the right thing to do, and it pays off.

32 If you can't handle challenges from within your team, you're not ready to handle the challenges from your competitors.

33 If you want people to watch your back, you have to watch theirs.

34 Loyalty is a two-way street. Be kind and flexible to staff and they'll return the favour.

35 Be the first to get stuck into something and don't be afraid to do the menial tasks.

36 Culture is what happens when the leader isn't looking.

37 Don't hire arseholes. If you do, get rid of them, quickly. They're toxic.

38 Think big. If you aim for the stars and you hit the moon, you'll still come out ahead.

39 Sometimes it's wise to be content with a smaller part of the bigger pie.

40 Train your leaders to be leaders. They may not stay with you forever, but they'll remember you forever.

41 $1 + 1 = 3$. The sum of the whole is bigger than the parts. You will be much stronger by collaborating with others than by doing it all on your own.

Part III
Full speed ahead

CHAPTER 12

It takes two

So, here we are in part III of a three-part book and we are yet to address the three questions we get asked all the time: 'How do you guys get along?', 'Who does what?' and 'How did you manage to achieve so much in just 13 years?'

Our first Catch employee, Vijay, who worked with us for 10 years and knows us well, said, 'This business would not have succeeded with two Gabbys or two Hezis'—and he was right. We have completely different strengths and weaknesses and, as it turns out, these differences have been very complementary.

People often say, 'If there are two founders and they always think alike, then one of them is not necessary', so on that count, we've been fortunate as we brought a diverse range of skills and perspectives to the business. While we drive each other mad every single day, the reality is those differences have worked well for us. We instinctively let the other take the lead when necessary. For example, Hezi is not passionate about logistics, while Gabby has never been interested in the workings of IT. Gabby loves traditional marketing. Hezi loves digital marketing. Gabby likes public speaking. Hezi prefers to be behind the scenes.

Building a business is demanding and can be an emotional rollercoaster, so having another person to share the pain and success with can be valuable and comforting. It enabled us to share the good cop/bad cop title on a weekly basis, which was a relief. No-one wants to be the bad cop all the time. Having two co-founders also enabled us to get a lot more done. As an entrepreneur, you have to make thousands of decisions every day. As a solo founder, by definition, you'll always be the smartest person in the room. But when you have two people with contrasting opinions debating the merits or otherwise of a decision, you almost always get a better result. A great partner will be invigorated by your strengths and will compensate for your weaknesses at the same time. Can you build a start-up on your own? Of course, but it's much easier, and more fun, doing it with someone.

Gabby

Even if you just look at it from the perspective of sharing the workload, it would have been close to impossible for us to do what we did on our own. When we decided to launch Scoopon in 2010, Hezi literally left the premises to build it from scratch. The truth is that Hezi hated the operational day-to-day running of the business, but he was excellent at the early days of forming and motivating a newly established team. His departure was made possible because I was able to take over the management of the booming Catchoftheday business, which was a role I loved, so that division of labour really suited us.

Hezi

While we often argued, the disagreements were always civil as we both knew that we loved the business, and that our opinions were coming from a place of good intentions. On the flip side, there were many things in our core DNA that we always agreed on and never argued about. These included hard work and having a very high appetite for risk. We are both very generous and never, ever argue about money, which is often a major cause of disagreements among founders. You can probably attribute that quality to being brothers and having the same upbringing and values.

Debates are good for business

So how did we resolve our differences? We kept on arguing until one of us gave up or managed to convince the other to go ahead. Sometimes we didn't resolve the argument, but we knew that if we both agreed strongly on a certain topic, we should pursue it with full force.

For example, we both believed that the Catch business should have a marketplace component. We didn't know how the marketplace would end up, or how it would affect our customers or suppliers, but we agreed that we would, at some stage, need to jump in the water and push hard to make that happen.

When Nati Harpaz (more on him later) joined the business in 2016, we pretty much ran it in a group of three, which was quite interesting and refreshing. But that didn't mean that two opinions would always beat a single opinion. It simply meant that there were as many as three strong opinions in the room, which was very welcome. Having said that, there were lots of scenarios where one of us beat the other two by having a fair and intelligent argument. We firmly believed that no one person had all the answers but by putting our heads together and collaborating, we would have a better chance of finding the right one.

We did it once. Can we do it again?

It's not every day you sell a business for nearly one billion dollars. But we had done it and we were thrilled with the result. After the deal was done and the dust had settled, we were left to answer a critical question: What do we do now? For us, the answer was simple. We went back to work. After all, EatNow was only one part of a larger puzzle and we had other parts to deal with.

Thirty of the EatNow team members moved to Sydney to join the operational team of Menulog. This meant the Catch and Scoopon teams working out of the old Adidas building suddenly had a bit more physical space, and one less business to worry about.

Not content to let grass grow under our feet, and buoyed by the buzz that the Menulog sale had created, we reached out to Nick Sims, the mergers and acquisition lead at Goldman Sachs who had facilitated the sale, to look at a similar opportunity for Catch. He and his team were well acquainted with the intricacies of our business, and knew what we had to offer. Most VCs usually have a three- to five-year timeline in which they want to see their investments provide a return. It had been five years since we had taken on investors so, while there was no real pressure by our investors to start looking at some sort of an exit for the group, it was the right sort of timeline for us to look into it.

Our brief to Nick from Goldman Sachs was broad:

> *Hey Nick, you achieved an unbelievable price for Menulog. We'd now like you to investigate the opportunities that are out there for Catch, and when we say 'opportunities' we mean anything and everything: an initial public offering (IPO), a full sale, a part sale, etc. The door is wide open!*

Nick and his team went to work, but after a year of conversations with a few parties it became clear that there wasn't enough interest out there for what we had to offer. To say this was ego-shattering for the founders and team is an understatement. How could *no-one* be interested in this award-winning, market-leading, innovative, profitable business? Everyone has 20/20 vision in hindsight, but we didn't have it at the time. What the market saw was a complicated web of inter-related but unconnected businesses.

At that point, Catch was operating two main businesses:

1. *a 'product' division:*

    - Catchoftheday

    - Mumgo

    - Grocery Run

2. *a 'services' division (Scoopon), which had three arms:*

    - product

    - services

    - travel.

At first glance, it's easy to understand why our business was confusing to the market. We had products, services and travel all under one roof. What potential acquirer would be interested in such a mish-mash? We couldn't think of a single potential suiter that had the in-house skills or the background to handle this mixed business. We knew we had a great business, but to the outsider peering in, we looked unfocused. At one stage, Myer expressed an interest in our e-commerce offering, but with the Scoopon and travel businesses included in the package, that deal went nowhere. In retrospect, we certainly made it difficult for anyone to show a real interest in us. The diversity of businesses in the group wasn't the only issue. We had three other major detractions that made us unattractive. We had:

- *no competitive point of difference.* Our travel arm, offered through Scoopon, was struggling to compete against market leaders such as Luxury Escapes. Everyone wants to back a winner and at that time, it was Luxury Escapes. We had to face the reality that our travel offering was not up to scratch and had no real point of difference.

- *no growth*. Our product business (excluding Scoopon) had grown somewhat, but not materially for three years. For example, we'd gone from revenue of $196 million in FY2013, to $201 million in FY2014 to $218 million for FY2015, and FY2016 wasn't tracking any higher. When investors look at acquiring a company, they want to see a hockey-stick graph, not a flat-line graph. Why would anyone invest in a company that isn't growing?

- *no idea*. To be honest, we felt like complete idiots for not noticing these deficits before engaging Goldman Sachs. We wasted a full year of our life trying to sell the business and missed many other opportunities along the way because of it.

What went wrong?

We had to take a good look at ourselves and reflect on how our vision had become so blinkered that we couldn't see the blind spots that were hampering our progress. We prided ourselves on being astute entrepreneurs with a flair for spotting the next trend, and yet here we were, unaware of how we were being seen by the market.

A major part of the problem was that we, the owners, had, for all intents and purposes, 'checked out' of the business.

As hands-on business owners, we had been involved in every major decision for more than a decade, and while we would have liked that involvement to continue, the reality was we had a management team at the helm and we had to let them get on with the job of managing the business as best they could.

In addition, having Goldman Sachs shop the business around meant that any potential buyer needed to know that Gabby and Hezi would not be part of the business moving forward. To ensure the 'optics' of that were consistent, we deliberately avoided attending key meetings and being part of the decision-making process. Every M&A (mergers and acquisition) adviser will tell you that when you're up for sale, the entire management team should lay low, keep an even keel and not make any bombastic moves. As co-founders, this advice was monumentally hard for us to follow. It's in our DNA to build, innovate and grow—we'd been doing it every day for 10 years—so to resist that urge and be content to do absolutely nothing, to not get involved and to stay mute, went against everything we stood for.

But alas, that is what we did. In effect, we took our hands off the steering wheel because we had to and, as you'll discover, we paid the price.

Here's a summary of what we believe we achieved in the year of 2016.

2016 Achievements

_____

_____

_____

_____

_____

_____

_____

_____

_____

_____

_____

_____

_____

_____

More 2016 Achievements

_____

_____

_____

_____

_____

_____

_____

_____

_____

_____

_____

_____

The financial year of 2016 will forever be remembered as Our Year of Nothing Achieved.

Unintended consequences

If we weren't actively involved in the day-to-day decision making of the business, you might be asking, what were we doing? Well, we weren't altogether idle.

 Hezi

Having been 'advised' to keep away from the office while the sales process was taking place, for the first time I decided to put a little bit more focus on my personal life, an area I had completely neglected for so many years. I was 36, married to the business all these years and thinking about what legacy I would leave. Up until that point, I had also done very little travel so I decided to kick back. Within a few months, I had met the love of my life, Lina, who I later married, and started a family. Gabby joined a start-up program in Israel, watched some soccer, travelled to a few countries and relaxed with his family.

In this self-enforced downtime, we discovered some home truths, one of them being that for every action (or inaction) there is an opposite reaction. It was abundantly clear that by us stepping out of the business for almost an entire year, we had created a reaction—and not a good one. The critical factor that had made Catch so disruptive and agile was our culture. And now, with us absent from the detail of running the business, that culture was suffering. Innovation had all but ceased, the once party-like atmosphere had disappeared, and the buzz that infused the place had long gone. Morale was at an all-time low and it showed up where it counted the most. The bottom line.

The one that got away

Once the sale of Menulog hit the media, we received an influx of investment opportunities from every man and his dog. Young and not so young start-ups approached us looking for money, mentoring or both. We were happy to help and keen to get involved in helping others fulfil their dreams.

The process of meeting founders, and hearing their stories, plans and dreams, is a very exciting one and we soon started investing in a bunch of local start-ups. Some have failed already, while many are still thriving. Our investments include Hipages, Tribe, RateMyAgent, Catapult, Vervoe, Fiverr, Bookwell and a bunch of others.

Here's the story of an investment opportunity you just have to hear about.

A 26-year-old guy called Nick reached out to us for a meeting. Not knowing what the meeting was about we reluctantly accepted and gave him the obligatory 30-minute coffee. He had built some financial solution software that he was trying to flog to Catchoftheday. While he had managed to convince 30 small companies to use his software, we hadn't heard of any of them. But Nick didn't just want us as a customer, he wanted us as an investor in his new company. Finance and fintech were certainly not our areas of expertise, and we were dubious whether Nick's tiny software start-up could go up against the likes of Visa, PayPal and the other established giants in the sector. We said, 'Thanks Nick, but it's not for us. Good luck.'

The company?

Afterpay.

Nick Molnar and Anthony Eisen, who are the nicest guys, went on to build one of Australia's most successful digital businesses and their company is valued at $20* billion today. Need we say more?

We still do coffees with lots of potential start-ups on a weekly basis. Hit us up if you think you are the next Nick.

Email us at: **nextnick@catchofthedecade.com**

---

* This figure changes daily. Every time we look, it's going up.

CHAPTER 13

A new era

By June 2016, it had become clear that the merger or sale we had hoped for would not happen. Why would it? Financially we were going backwards, the year ahead was expected to be even worse and the family culture we had worked so hard to build had seen better days. We knew that the train we were driving was about to hit the wall, and that we as the co-drivers had to make a decision. Do we turn right, left or do nothing at all and plough straight into it? We were in a precarious position and a decision had to be made.

Q: What do we do next?

A: We jump back in and get our hands dirty, fully determined to bring the business back to where it rightfully belonged: at the top of the e-commerce tree.

Nati Harpatz, why don't you take it from here and tell them the story?

Nati

I'd met Gabby over the years at various retail events, and we shared a common language, cultural background and love of retail, so we understood each other and had an instant rapport. We met for a beer and he confided in me his concerns, frustrations and ideas going forward. I went away mulling over what he'd told me and sent him an email the next day containing a draft business plan proposing what the Catch management team could do to get back on track. To be honest, I thought this proposal might lead to a one-off consulting gig and that would be it, but Gabby has very strong instincts and had other ideas. Not long after I sent the email, he rang me and said, 'Come to Melbourne and meet with me and my brother'.

I jumped on a plane and spent a day talking to the brothers about how they could reinvigorate the business. That day turned into a week. We spent the time digging deep into all the operational, financial and cultural issues that were plaguing the business. Whatever I said or did in those meetings must have resonated because at the end of the week, they said to me, 'We think that you are the guy to lead the company into this new era. You should be our new CEO.'

To this day, it amazes me that they took the risk of parachuting me into a role that was clearly bigger than anything I had ever done before, but I guess that's just part of the Leibovich magic. They make decisions quickly and they generally get them right. That week of brainstorming the business was instrumental in creating the foundation for how we would move the organisation forward, and it all hinged on two critical elements.

1. *We needed to start now.*

The brothers wanted me to start immediately, which would have been fine if it were just me and I had nothing else on and lived down the road. But I had a young family, lived in Sydney and was a co-partner in a successful media business. But when the Leibovich's want you, they want you (and this once-in-a-lifetime opportunity was too good to refuse), so I handed the keys to my business partner, relocated my family to Melbourne and within one week, was at my desk, ready to start work. The brothers made the move as seamless as possible. When we moved into the house, it was filled with everything a young family could want: toys, games, appliances, towels, sheets, the works! All courtesy of Catch, of course.

2. *We needed to control our destiny.*

For change to occur quickly, tough and maybe unpopular decisions would need to be made. We would need to take big risks and buy back control of the business so that we were only accountable to ourselves. This meant buying out the external shareholders. Gabby and Hezi had good relationships with their shareholders and didn't want to do the wrong thing by them. This would need to be done amicably and fairly.

To be honest, Hezi wasn't so keen on putting almost all his money back into the business and risking it on a 'green CEO' with an A4 page business plan, but for some reason, after a few days, Gabby got him over the line. I don't know what he said to him, but it worked.

 **Gabby and Hezi**

It also became clear that we needed to get more 'hands on' again. At this stage our business was 11 years old. Our leadership team was composed of many of the people who had helped us build the business from day one. These were individuals who had joined us in their early twenties, and in most cases had never really worked elsewhere. A decade at the same work place is a long time, and some felt they had taken Catchoftheday as far as they could and were ready for some new challenges.

In the first couple of months after Nati's arrival, we changed seven out of the top 10 C-level people and introduced a new group of executives who had the attitude, energy and experience to restore the business to its former glory. This did not come without cost, heartache and a lot of soul searching. Exiting people from management roles is fraught with difficulty. Not only do you lose momentum, you lose knowledge. Our key concern was that with so many senior executives leaving the building at the same time, their corporate and operational know-how would exit along with them. We knew this would happen but trusted that the people who remained had the knowledge and skills to keep things moving. No-one is indispensable. After all, the cemetery is filled with irreplaceable people!

Now that the issue of whether the business would be sold or not was resolved, many of our team were able to assess their future with more clarity. This was good for everyone as it was time for a change and it gave us the chance to re-imagine what the future might look like and who would be the right people to take us there.

We started the new era by hiring new teams of digitally savvy professionals holding deep expertise in e-commerce. We were a significant business, turning over millions every week, and we needed senior team players who could identify, harness and convert the opportunities ahead of us. Importantly, we needed to ensure that those new team members would embody the Catch culture we had worked so hard to create in the first place.

Transforming the Catch culture

Nati

US management consultant Peter Drucker says 'culture eats strategy for breakfast'—and it's true. Strategy is important, but without a strong culture and a strong team, even the best strategy will fail, and with our culture at an all-time low, we knew that we had to address it before anything else, or with the best will in the world, the change management process would fail.

No-one likes change and the first thing a new CEO will do is bring change. To transform a business, you need to give people the confidence that it can be done. This can be achieved with quick wins and other actions that create momentum and value. It needs to be physical and real, as early as possible and include everyone so they can quickly start to believe in what will be delivered.

To get the ball rolling, I set up a comprehensive series of staff interviews. I've discovered that if you ask the people who work in the trenches what's wrong with the business, they will generally tell you. They'll also tell you how to fix it. These forums made it possible for everyone to contribute openly without fear of repercussions, and enabled them to debate the idea as if their lives depended on it and then forget all about it, have a drink together and stay good friends. We had a lot of diversity in our team, which was really important and helpful as it meant we collected a wide range of opinions and created lots of options for how to do things differently.

The interviews also helped us understand what was going on and why things weren't working as well as they should. My strategy for bringing out the best in people is to empower them to be their best. I believe a good manager should unleash the reins that hold people back so they can be free to make fast, effective decisions. To achieve this, I established a series of core values and operating principles via a process I called 'building the clock'. 'Telling the time' is when everyone relies on you to tell the time. 'Building the clock' means that everyone is capable of telling the time at any time so they can make decisions independently. For change to happen, leaders need to be empowered and set up for success.

The clock concept empowered the team to make decisions without solely relying on management, and that was the secret to bringing back the culture that had made the business so unique in the first place. With the shackles off, the team transformed. Coupled with a strong sense of purpose, a 'get shit done' attitude and a willingness to make big decisions on the run, we started to punch well above our weight. We had 200 office staff at the time, but we did the work of 400 and each and every one of them felt they were a part of the journey.

This style of consultative management doesn't work for everyone, but it worked for Catch. If the truth be known, it suited my personality too. People often tell me that I change my mind frequently, and it's true. I am actually proud of that because it means I am open to being changed. If someone presents me with a better argument that proves that my previous assumption is wrong, I will adopt that idea without hesitation. By doing so, I remove ego from the decision-making process. I believe that when everyone makes decisions on the basis of merit, rather than seniority, we all benefit.

By taking advice and sharing my thoughts with the team I managed to get the first part of the strategy underway. The team was on board, they trusted us enough to tell us the truth and they were open to implementing the changes we had discussed, most of which had come from them anyway!

The second thing we needed to do was attract new customers. (The brothers already had a pivotal idea planned for that. More about that later.) While the existing range of products and offerings had served us well for a decade, the reality was that customers wanted more options, diversity and range. Yes, our customers loved us and they were loyal, but if we wanted them to remain loyal, we had to give them a good reason to be loyal. Expanding the range would be a start, and this would in turn help us reach more people.

> **WHEN EVERYONE MAKES DECISIONS ON THE BASIS OF MERIT, RATHER THAN SENIORITY, WE ALL BENEFIT.**

The final recommendation our team made was simple, but important. This sounds frivolous but if you were to ask the team what they most remember about my arrival back in 2016, they'll say, 'he brought us coffee'. Being based in suburban Mulgrave, 26 kilometres south of Melbourne, there were few cafés around so the team had to make do with Nescafé. We could have installed an automated coffee machine, but we went a step further and set up a café in our foyer offering barista-style coffee and it was a huge success! Such a simple thing, but so appreciated.

Gabby and Hezi have always been a dynamic duo, but now we were making decisions as a trio and that meant we each had to fight and debate to have our point of view heard and accepted. The best argument normally won and we could move forward knowing that each decision made had been road tested and kicked around enough for us to know it stood a reasonable chance of being right. And Gabby's well-known predisposition for putting on a party to mark any win, birthday or award, also helped recreate the celebratory, fun-loving culture the brothers had worked so hard to create all those years earlier.

Nati, Gabby and Hezi: Getting shit done

Have a start-up mindset (even when you're not a start-up)

It always amazes us when we see young start-ups spending huge amounts of money (often investors' funds) on office fit-outs and a bunch of unnecessary roles that could easily be accommodated from within.

Even when we were making millions, we retained our start-up mentality, mainly because we really despise wastage. For example, when Nati stepped into the Adidas office and wanted to change some of the signage, he grabbed a tin of paint and a roller and got to work. When we opened our Chadstone retail store, we'd drive around collecting stuff to be ready in time for the grand opening. This kind of behaviour may sound unusual coming from the leadership team of a 500-person operation, but that is exactly the kind of behaviour that tells the team that even though we are a large company, we still have a start-up mindset, and that's the way it will continue. This 'can do' attitude flows through to the team and makes them cost conscious (so you don't have to keep reinforcing the message).

Back on track

Now that we were back on board and steering, it was time to set the sails and the coordinates that would take us to the next destination. Getting Tiger Global and the other investors on board was critical to us moving back into the business again. They owned 40 per cent of the group, they were our partners and we could only do it with their approval. But what would they say? What if they said no?

We needn't have worried. Tiger Global, Lee Fixel and our other investors were fully supportive of the plan. We'd been in constant communication with them throughout 2016 and they were aware of the financial and cultural issues we were facing. Compared to their investments in behemoths like JD.com, Alibaba and Facebook we were a tiny blip on their horizon, but they were super accommodating and supportive of our desire to take the reins back and become a 'family' company again.

We reached an agreement on a price that, as they say, 'both parties were a little bit unhappy with', and got back to business.

The buy-back deal surprised many of our close friends and colleagues. They asked, 'Why would the founders take a large sum of money out of their own pocket to buy back a business they were themselves struggling to grow?' It was a good question but, as ever, we relied on our instincts and pushed on. You'll never see us gambling at the casino but this was without doubt *the* riskiest and *the* biggest bet we had ever made. We may have looked confident, but we felt anything but. When our colleagues questioned our decision, we said, 'Talk to us in three years, and you'll discover if we're really smart or really stupid'.

Congratulations for reading this far.

You've earned yourself a coffee break!

In the meantime, check out this website:

Carousale.com

Don't forget to always be selling.

CHAPTER 14

Time for some major changes

The pace of life was increasing. With the Tiger deal done and dusted, and the team transformation well underway, it was time to turn our attention to the issue of growth.

FY2016 was the first year in our history that our product revenue, excluding Scoopon, had actually gone backwards (from $218 million to $187 million). How were we going to change this downward trend? The team had told us what they thought. Now we had to do something about it. But how? We were constrained by two critical factors: dollars and space. Put simply, the financial and physical resources we needed to grow were both in short supply.

We interrogated every aspect of the business and decided that Scoopon, and in particular Scoopon Travel, provided a great opportunity for growth. Luxury Escapes was our big competitor at the time and they were killing it, and us. Since their arrival on the scene a few years earlier, they had well and truly established themselves as the darling of the travel industry. They'd formed great relationships with hotel chains and airlines, and offered the mum-and-dad traveller time-limited luxury travel packages at bargain prices (similar to the Catch model we'd pioneered a decade earlier, but for travel).

The founders of Luxury Escapes, Adam Schwab and Jeremy Same, were two switched-on digital entrepreneurs. We initially spotted them when they launched Zoupon.com.au, a competitor to Scoopon (how dare they!) back in mid 2010. They then ended up buying the Cudo website from Channel Nine, as well as the Australian franchise for LivingSocial. In 2013, they rebranded and called themselves Lux Group and launched Luxuryescapes.com.au shortly thereafter. (A great name, by the way!)

While we liked the guys and were impressed with their Catch-like chutzpah and energy, we didn't let sentiment get in the way of business. We went head to head against them and did our best to take market share off them, but no matter what we did, we couldn't make a dent. Without a clear point of difference, we just couldn't cut through the clutter. Playing second fiddle to the first mover was not new territory to us. When we launched EatNow we bugged the shit out of Menulog so badly they decided that merging would be easier than competing. Maybe we could do the same here? Could lightning strike twice? We decided to find out.

If you can't join them, beat them

In 2015 we had had some exploratory conversations with Lux Group in regards to a potential merger of some of our entities, but sadly we were unable to agree on terms. Remember, one of the rules that defines a great buyer is 'Keep the door open', so we kept the door open, had regular catchups at the South Melbourne market with Adam and Jeremy and separately continued growing our respective businesses.

When Nati joined us in the latter part of 2016, we thought we might as well try a bit harder to beat them. After all, we knew everything there was to know about the travel sector. We had Jon Beros and his Scoopon Travel team eager to innovate and keep the spark alive, so in early 2017, just five months after Nati's arrival, we gave Jon the full authority and financial backing to go and build our own luxury travel brand. We decided that if you can't join them, then you should do your best to beat them.

We called it Bonvoyage.com.au—a pretty cool name, hey?

You don't have what I want!

The next order of business concerned Catch. We had to face the reality that our star performer had stalled. On the surface we looked strong. The business generated roughly $200 million a year in sales, and the warehouse was filled to the brim with $40 million worth of stock and more than 30 000 products on offer. This may sound like a lot, but compared with eBay, which offered hundreds of millions of listings, we were tiny. And that was our problem.

We didn't have to look too far from home to find out what was wrong. When we asked our wives why they weren't buying more from Catch, they had the same reply, 'You don't have what I want'. Never a truer word was spoken—and from someone in our own home! They were right. We simply did not stock enough products in enough categories. It was a bitter realisation, but a lightbulb moment too. How could it have taken us this long to notice something so obvious? But what was the solution? We remembered what Jeff Bezos, the founder of Amazon, had said years earlier: 'Marketplaces are eating the world'. We had often discussed adding a marketplace component to the Catch site but we were always too busy or the timing wasn't right, or the IT department was too busy, or ... there was always a reason. Now we had no excuse.

WE WEREN'T AS BUSY AND THE TIMING WAS RIGHT. WE HAD TO STOP THINKING AND START DOING.

CHAPTER 15

The marketplace beckons

For the uninitiated, a marketplace is a website where sellers congregate to offer their goods to an aggregated audience. Amazon, eBay, Alibaba, Airbnb and Uber are all marketplaces, and you could say they've all been reasonably successful. We had our own marketplace with Menulog, and that worked pretty well for us, too. In 2020, the word on every marketer's lips was 'marketplace'. Other than COVID-19, it was the hottest topic in town. Every industry needs a marketplace and every entrepreneur wants to own one. The only trouble is, you need big bucks, and even bigger balls, to build one. They're not for the faint-hearted. Creating a marketplace made sense for a multitude of reasons. It stacked up strategically and solved a lot of issues. It was a:

- *capital-light model*. This meant we could offer more products without needing to buy more products, add more warehouse space or hire more packing staff.

- *scalable model*. If we didn't need to buy the goods, we didn't need to photograph, pack and ship them either. We could add millions of new products without adding overheads, and run the entire marketplace operation on a shoestring.

- *compelling offer*. If we offered more products, we attracted more shoppers, which generated more traffic, which increased sales. If we increased sales, we attracted more suppliers, at which point, the network effect* would kick in.

- *destination website*. After a decade of attracting the shopper with 'surprise' deals, we could now attract the 'intent shopper' (a customer who comes to you searching for something specific).

For these and many other reasons, the three of us debated long and hard and agreed that we'd step off the cliff and commit to what would be one of the riskiest, most complicated and expensive decisions we had ever made. We would launch a marketplace. In business parlance, making critical decisions like this is known as 'pivoting'. This was a big one. We made it in June 2016 and we knew it would be a massive inflection point in our business.

Amazon is coming

On the cusp of committing significant dollars and energy to the launch of our marketplace, we heard a very disturbing rumour that the Goliath of them all—Amazon, no less—was coming to Australia. Amazon! The number one marketplace in the Western world was coming here. We contemplated the enormity of what we were doing—going head to head against Amazon—and we'd be lying if we said we didn't consider giving up on the idea. But as we've always said, if we have an idea by midnight, we execute by midday, and this was no different. We figured we might be tiny by comparison, but on this occasion, we were the incumbent, our customers and suppliers loved us, and we had a database of millions of happy customers who (we hoped) would choose us over our American counterpart.

---

* The network effect is a phenomenon whereby increased numbers of people or participants improve the value of a good or service. For example, take Uber and Airbnb. The more people who use the site, the more useful the site becomes to other people. The more useful it becomes, the more people use it. And so on.

But we knew we'd have to act fast. Amazon was in our rear mirror, closing in fast and the clock was ticking. Having the 'first mover advantage' is an asset, but as everyone knows when it comes to Amazon, anything can happen.

The race is on

In theory, launching a brand-new marketplace sounds easy. In reality, it's extremely complicated. Just finding a team to build the marketplace itself was challenging. Our first instinct, as always, was to build it in-house, but our team of 30+ IT professionals told us in no uncertain terms, 'No way! We're too busy building the Bon Voyage website. Go away.'

We searched high and low to find a software company that could manage this mammoth task, and preferably one that was already building marketplace platforms. Why reinvent the wheel, right? We moved quickly, and after an intensive global search, located a SAAS (Software as a Service) company called Mirakl based in France that specialised in building retail marketplace software. What a miracle! Within 48 hours, we had signed the contract. Adrien Nussenbaum, the CEO and co-founder, was shocked we made such a major decision so quickly. He said, 'Working with Catch has been a wonderful experience from day one. Their trust in Mirakl recommendations and high ambitions made for a powerful combination'. We were as happy to find them as they were to find us, and we celebrated into the night with a few drinks. Très bien! Nati swears his school-boy French helped clinch the deal. We're not so sure.

> **BUT WE KNEW WE'D HAVE TO ACT FAST. AMAZON WAS IN OUR REAR MIRROR, CLOSING IN FAST AND THE CLOCK WAS TICKING.**

Make no mistake. This move was a big gamble for us. Some people around us said, 'Don't do it! You're mad! You can't win!' We realised that pivoting the business model was a massive risk. Business builders often find themselves in situations where they need to make 80 per cent of their decisions with only 20 per cent visibility. Being an entrepreneur is about playing the odds. We'd done it before, we could do it again. This newly formed management team of three were on a mission to prove everyone wrong, to turn this business around and to make this marketplace a success.

More questions than answers

In the spirit of our newly-found culture of collaboration and open discussion, we asked the team for their input. We gathered all the relevant people around the table to discuss the operational components of adding a marketplace to the Catch business, and while we had their interest and enthusiasm, we certainly didn't have everyone's support. All decisions as crucial as this are accompanied by vigorous debate and discussion, and this was a critical decision that everyone had an opinion on. We remember these meetings as being pretty explosive because everyone was concerned about how this new development would affect them. We compiled a list of questions, concerns and complexities; questions that would need quick answers if we were to have any chance of success. It became clear the marketplace could function in many different ways and do many different things. We just needed to decide what they were, and how we would achieve them. Here are just a few of the questions we had to ask ourselves:

- Who decides what sellers should be admitted to the marketplace?

- Do we mention the seller's name when displaying the products?

- How many sellers should compete for the same product?
- If a product is sold on both Catch and the marketplace, do Catch products get priority?
- Should we allow sellers to beat Catch on pricing?
- Should we accept sellers from overseas?
- What categories should we offer first?
- Who do we hire to run the marketplace?
- How do we maintain our levels of Catch customer service if we're not servicing the customer?
- How quickly should a seller dispatch an item?
- How many employees do we hire to launch the marketplace team?

The list of questions was nearly as long as this book, but the common thread that connected them all was the recognition that we had built a tremendous brand over 11 years; that we stood for something; that we had strong values in place; and that we weren't prepared to compromise on any of them.

If we were to pursue a marketplace, it needed to retain the DNA we had developed at Catch.

It had to represent everything we stood for: great prices, excellent customer service and fast shipping…and fun. If that was the answer, then there was really only one question: 'How do we add a marketplace, introduce thousands of new sellers under the Catch brand, and still maintain the Catch culture?' This question of course led to another. If the marketplace must represent the Catch culture, what exactly *is* the Catch culture? Defining culture is like catching a cloud.

But with the new team in place, we thought it was time to document this nebulous concept so that we could enshrine it as part of our corporate values, and hold it up for future generations of Catch employees to look at for guidance and inspiration. We called these values the 'Catch DNA'. These were the commandments that underpinned it.

The 10 Commandments of the Catch Culture

We:

1. *Out-think the competition and execute faster!*

Having great ideas is just the beginning. It's all about taking these ideas and turning them into profitable businesses. We have never been too corporate, which has allowed us to act fast once we have that special lightbulb moment!

2. *Create ongoing win-win relationships with our suppliers.*

Without your suppliers, you are nothing. Never forget that! From our first deal to our last, we've always thought long-term. For that reason, you should never have a 'hit and run' mentality. Suppliers are part of your business. If they are upset, they will never be back, and worse, they'll tell their friends.

3. *Look for new ways to delight our customers.*

Without customers, you are nothing. Our core business was always about selling people things that they didn't plan to buy, which meant a lot of repeat purchasing. Our customers love us for many reasons, but at the end of the day they need to love the products they paid for with their hard-earned cash. We all love unwrapping that parcel and trying on a pair of shoes with that 'brand new' smell, but let us tell you, those shoes smell a lot better when you've just saved $80 on them.

4. *Work hard, but have lots of fun as well.*

To be successful you need to work hard, but rest assured, if your workmates are your friends and you look forward to seeing them each day, you'll enjoy coming to work and be a lot more productive. We strived to create a fun environment. In addition to the state-of-the-art building we worked in, we had a gym, basketball court, barbecues, bicycles and a giant slide. We also held themed celebrations like pyjama parties and Halloween days where you could let your hair down and have a drink.

5. *Grow through positive word of mouth.*

We are very proud to say that in our first few years of business, we didn't spend any money on marketing. Our positive word of mouth came from great deals and outstanding customer service. Everyone loves to show off their latest purchase, and the recommendation is even more convincing when you can tell your friends how much you've saved on that latest toy or dress.

6. *Listen to everyone and value everyone's opinion.*

We were never dictators. What we, and our staff, loved about working at Catch was that anyone, no matter who they were or what part of the business they worked in, had access and the ability to change our future direction. We encouraged collaboration, hired from within, and gave our staff the opportunities to contribute and the tools to grow.

7. *Coach rather than criticise.*

We treated our team like family and like all functional families, they succeed with love, not criticism. While we started with a small 'family' of seven, which grew to 400+, we tried hard to make everyone feel that their contribution was critical to the overall success of the business.

8. *Don't wear suits.*

This may not be a core value of our company but it's really important to us. We personally hate suits and save them for weddings only. Work is not a wedding ceremony; work is about being yourself and allowing your creativity to burst out. How can it burst out if you're all stiff?

9. *Don't over-spend.*

Start-ups don't have spare cash to spend on nonsense, and as such need to develop a good sense of fund allocation.

It's true we are really no longer what people like to call a start-up, but with more than seven different websites, we are very happy to say that our large and active office continues to behave and budget like a start-up. We never let our company become a CRAP company: a **c**ompany that can't **r**ealise **a p**rofit.

10. *Think outside the box. Think differently.*

If you want what you've always had, do what you've always done. If you want something to be different, you have to be, think or act differently from what the others are doing. Don't always accept the obvious answer.

11. *Are kind and humble.**

No explanation required.

How we built the marketplace

We could have debated the merits of the marketplace for months on end and still not gotten everyone on board, so we did what we've always done and jumped right in and said, 'Let's do it!'

Did we have all the answers on how it would get done? No way. We didn't even have the questions! But we figured it was better to be in the game than watch from the sidelines. The one thing we all agreed on was that we would have a curated marketplace. We did not want to be an open marketplace like eBay or Amazon where anyone could sell anything for any price. We wanted to control who would sell on our site and what products they would sell. We also wanted to ensure all the sellers could maintain high standards of customer service and ship as fast as we could. The

---

* Yes, we have 11 commandments. Break the rules if you want to.

mission that drove our every action and our every decision was to always give the customer what they wanted: a great range at the best prices.

Creating a curated marketplace not only solved the quality issue, it also enabled us to create a point of difference from eBay and Amazon. If you go to eBay and search for a black iPhone case, you'll be presented with hundreds of sellers offering the same items. But who do you trust? Who's reliable? Who's got the best price? You have so many choices you end up not buying anything at all. It's death by a thousand decisions. We didn't want this for our marketplace, and creating a curated marketplace meant we would avoid it.

We put our team of 60 product hunters on the job to start sifting through the sellers we wanted to invite onto the marketplace. They were the smartest, most experienced product source-ers in the country. They had their work cut out for them because everyone who was anyone wanted to be on our marketplace. We took our cues from the John West school of product selection—'it's the products we reject that make us the best'—and eventually turned away 80 per cent of the sellers who applied to be on the marketplace.

This marketplace offered us unparalleled opportunity to expand our offering. With our deal-of-the-day model, we had been limited in what we could sell as it had to meet a range of criteria.

Now, the shackles were off and we could offer almost anything.

The size and weight of products were no longer an issue so we could offer furniture, gym equipment, trampolines, bathroom products and camping gear. We could be as niche as we wanted and offer obscure, long tail products that were of interest only to a few; we could offer products that had an endless range, such as books, jewellery, cosmetics and apparel. Big ticket items such as high-end electronics, designer watches and luxury goods were also now on offer. The world was our oyster!

THIS MARKETPLACE OFFERED US UNPARALLELED OPPORTUNITY TO EXPAND OUR OFFERING.

One of the first companies to join our marketplace was booktopia.com.au, Australia's most successful and largest bookseller. The founder, Tony Nash, and the deputy CEO, Wayne Baskin, are seasoned retailers, and they jumped at the opportunity to offer their range of 100 000+ books to the Catch audience. Catch had never really offered books before and certainly had no intentions of stocking 100 books, let alone as many as 100 000, so this was another great example of win-win-win. Booktopia sells more books to new Catch customers, Catch sells more books (1000 every day) and the consumer is super happy to discover a product on Catch that they weren't expecting to find. Everyone is happy!

The launch of BonVoyage.com.au

BON **VOYAGE**

While the build-up to the launch of the marketplace was taking shape, the travel team and Jon Beros were still working hard on building the Bon Voyage business. Luxury Escapes, being the market leader, had the first mover advantage. As a late arrival to the scene we had to launch with a bang and quickly get as many eyeballs as we could on our new site. We'd enjoyed our experience having Jason Alexander as our brand ambassador for Catch and thought we could duplicate the strategy and find an equally compelling ambassador to launch Bon Voyage. We chose Jennifer Hawkins, a former Miss Universe, a celebrity everyone in Australia loved and respected.

The Bon Voyage team and our lovely ambassador, Jennifer Hawkins.

Launching any business from scratch is hard to do, but launching one with the backing of the Catch group made the job so much easier. It meant Bon Voyage could tap into the customer service, design, IT, marketing and finance functionalities that already existed and leverage the substantial databases of Catch and Scoopon. Through Scoopon Travel we already had all the relationships with the hotels and resorts, so getting great product flow wasn't a problem either. We remarketed our offering via banners and daily emails, and took a leaf out of the Luxury Escapes playbook by creating vibrant, four-colour, full-page newspaper advertisements, which had worked so well for them.

Our first deal put us on the map. We collaborated with Melbourne's five-star Crown Casino to offer 10 000 room nights and we sold out within 24 hours. Our team continued to source unbeatable deals like this and within a very short space of time Bon Voyage became a big blip on the radar of the market leader and started to threaten the territory it had begun to think it owned. In short, our activities and awareness were starting to bite and Luxury Escapes were beginning to get just a little bit annoyed, which was just what we wanted.

What's in a name?

By July 2017, Catchoftheday was more than 11 years old. We were an established business with a high media profile, millions of customers and hundreds of employees. We'd moved offices more times than we cared to remember, bought and sold many businesses along the way, and changed our business model multiple times to reflect the changes in the market and the customers we served.

The one thing that hadn't changed, however, was our name: Catch of the Day. While we loved our name and logo, and recognised that it had worked so well for us for so long, the (sad) reality was that with the marketplace about to launch, the name no longer reflected what we did, or what we offered. For example, while our site had 30 000 products on it every single day, we were about to add an extra million+ products via the marketplace, so the name 'Catch of the Day' would quickly become redundant. This forced us to ask ourselves this question: Why are we still called Catch of the Day?

THERE WAS ONLY ONE SOLUTION. WE HAD TO REBRAND.

After a decade of success, here we were, about to mess with the name that had done so much to put us on the map. We were super conscious of the risk that messing with the brand posed. Under Nati's cultural revolution, we had hired Ryan Gracie, one of Australia's most energetic and experienced retail marketers. The original plan was for him to come in for only a few weeks to help us get our marketing back on track, but we convinced him to stay. It was a good move for all involved. With decades in the business working for the likes of JB Hi-Fi and Fantastic Toys we knew he was well placed to lead this very important change.

While it sounded easy in theory, the task of rebranding an entire organisation as diverse as ours took hours of long, detailed discussions. Choosing the name going forward was a given. We had been referred to as 'Catch' and calling ourselves 'Catch' for as long as we could remember, so in many ways Catch of the Day *was* Catch.

Deciding on the new logo was a little harder. Do we go with a revolution and start from scratch? Or do we go for an evolution and make a subtle change? We went with the revolution, enlisted our own creative team, ran staff competitions, as we always did, and even used 99Designs and Fiverr to crowdsource some options. Everyone had a crack!

The launch of the new brand came with mixed emotions but the roll-out went smoothly and now, when we look at the new Catch logo, we have to say that we love it as much as we loved the original. Even now, years after the rebrand, we are thrilled to see the new Catch logo on billboards around town and know we made the right decision. Old habits die hard though. We're still referred to by our customers, the media and the industry in general as the founders of Catch of the Day. Some things will never change, and that's just fine with us!

Ryan Gracie, Gabby and Hezi. It was Mexican day at the Catch office.

A masterclass in how to build a memorable brand

Ryan Gracie is the chief marketing officer at Catch and was previously in a similar role at JB Hi-Fi, so he knows a thing or two about marketing, digital and branding. We asked him to share his thoughts about his time at Catch and what made our branding so successful.

In business, brand is everything. Having a brand means having people who think of you first when it's time to purchase, who feel bad for betraying you, and who trust and support you no matter what. To succeed in business, you need people to fall in love with your brand. The bigger your brand, the more loyal customers you will have.

So how do you grow your brand?

Constantly communicating with your current customers through highly targeted communication is smart, but it's not enough. You need to reach new customers through mass communication. If your business is hooked on the lower funnel, performance marketing drug, well, that's kind of okay, but you need to counterbalance that hit with an entire funnel strategy. Top of funnel brand activity must not be neglected for short-term sales results or your business will be on that drug forever.

There are six key elements to growing your brand:

1. *become famous for all the right reasons*
2. *be memorable and recognisable by codifying all of your brand assets*
3. *define what you stand for*
4. *decide what is your customer value proposition*
5. *nominate the problem you will solve*
6. *identify the customer need you will meet, and then communicate it consistently and relentlessly.*

Don't be afraid to say the same thing over and over again. Remember, branding is a form of brainwashing, and because consumers generally make fast, unconscious decisions based on emotions, you need to continually drive your message, your look and your feel through your communications.

Your biggest fans, and those who never shop with you, should both be able to see your advertisement and know at a glance who you are and what you stand for. To achieve this, strive to ensure your campaign branding looks consistent, and uses the same tone of voice. By the way, don't hide your logo. Make it big, make it bold and make it burn into the minds of your customers.

Buying sales through performance marketing works if you always have a positive Return On Ad Spend (ROAS), but until you are on the consumers' consideration list and mentally available, you will have to pay for their love through performance marketing forever. This is not sustainable and leads to a point of diminishing returns.

At Catch it wasn't always about winning with great products at great prices. While price was our point of difference, we also knew we had to win them over with personality, a sense of 'theatre', and by creating a holistic shopping 'experience' that was exciting, surprising and fun. Your customer value proposition must be compelling, engaging and unique, so steer clear of completely copying your competitors. Find their weakness, find a territory you can own and take it off them.

While the big global brands often allocate around 60 per cent of their marketing budget on long-term brand building activity and 40 per cent on short-term sales activation campaigns, we didn't adhere to that strategy at Catch, and it was a mistake not to do so. It's easy to see how we fell into this trap of preferencing the short term over the long term. Brand-building activity is not easily measured and sales can't be directly attributed to a billboard or a radio commercial, so it's a harder investment case to make. Branding often feels like a waste of money at the time as the hit is not instant, but if you have the courage to invest in it, the delayed hit is much more potent and long-lasting.

A strong brand is your best defence against competitors and your most valuable asset. Brand building takes long-term investment, and there is no instant return, but the return comes in the months and years following when your brand is famous, your customers love you and they demonstrate that love by coming to you first, frequently spending their money with you and telling their friends. That's how you build a memorable brand.

Here are a few of the logos we considered for the Catch rebrand.

The side benefits of building a big brand

Gabby

There are some amusing side benefits to building a business. Seeing your brand sit alongside some of the biggest brands in the world is one of them. You know those gift cards you pick up at Coles and Woolworths when you've forgotten (or can't be bothered) to buy a present for someone? Yeah, those. Well, as a result of our brand building campaigns, we created a Catch gift card and were delighted to see it displayed on the carousel alongside cards from Netflix, Apple, eBay and more. We got a buzz every time we saw it there. It reminded us of where we'd started and how far we'd come. Don't tell anyone, but whenever my kids and I find ourselves in these shops, we 're-merchandise' the gift cards and move the Catch card from the bottom row to prime position at eye level. You gotta do what you gotta do! I'll always be a proud Catcher.

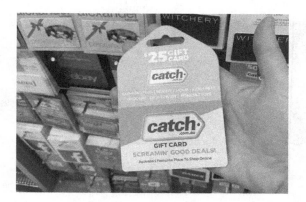

We got a kick out of seeing our Catch-branded gift cards in the big retail stores.

The gamble paid off

We launched the marketplace in July 2017 and the results were beyond anyone's expectations. In our first week of trade, the marketplace generated 917 new orders. By week four, it had doubled to 1800 orders, and by week eight we were taking 5000 orders. Within three months, the site was generating more than $2 million every week. We couldn't believe our eyes. Revenue was growing at rates that we had never experienced, and we were now on track to reach $50 million in sales by the end of our first year.

We said to each other,

'We should have done this earlier!'

While we were super pleased with the results, we couldn't help but think how much we could have made if we'd expanded our offering earlier. Little things caught our attention, such as costumes. In one day, we sold 300 costumes! Who'd have thought? Imagine if we'd been selling costumes from the beginning? What a missed opportunity!

We were onto a winner again. Luck? Who knows, but fortune favours the brave and the massive gamble we took in launching the marketplace had paid off in spades. We weren't the only winners. Our 500+ sellers were beneficiaries too, selling so much more and introducing their product and brand to a whole new audience.

Here's a message to all the arrogant brands out there still sitting on the fence wondering if you should join our (or any other) marketplace:

You need to be where the customer is! You need to sell your product on other marketplaces. Remember: 1+1=3 !

Our customers were the ultimate winners because they could now take their pick from a vast array of Australia's best suppliers at the best prices.

Amazon is getting closer

While the marketplace was flying, we had our eye well and truly on the Goliath across the Atlantic. We knew it was coming, we just didn't know when. We'd heard Amazon had secured a 24 000 m² fulfilment centre in Melbourne and while the media were quick to suggest that our Catch star would burn brightly and then crash and burn the minute Amazon arrived, we didn't see it that way. We genuinely believed that a rising tide floats all boats and that Amazon's arrival would increase the awareness of online shopping and we'd be the recipient of that extra attention.

We had built great relationships with our suppliers, had a truckload of them waiting to get on the platform and knew they wouldn't desert us the minute Amazon arrived. Our customers loved that we were a little Aussie start-up that had made good, that we were approachable and that we communicated with them in a fun and personable way. With Amazon on the horizon, we hoped this sentiment would help position us as a genuine alternative to them, even if our product range was a fraction of theirs. We'd been the number two player in many markets and each had worked out just fine. We hoped that this would be no different.

Don't chase a rabbit down a hole

You'd have thought that with the launch of the marketplace and Bon Voyage we would have been content with the status quo. Sales were going great, revenues were up and awareness was at an all-time high. Surely, maybe now we could stop for a moment and smell the roses? But nah. We've never been happy with the status quo. We were always looking for the next bright, shiny object, and we saw it in Pumpkin Patch.

Pumpkin Patch was a 40-plus-year-old children's clothing brand. It requires little introduction. Our kids wore it with pride over the years. One sunny day in 2017 Pumpkin Patch went out of business and into receivership. You may have seen it. It was front page news. Sadly, we seem to see more and more retailers over the past few years throw in the towel like this. But we thought we could do something with the brand, so Nati, Hezi, Gabby and our ever-reliable CFO Mark Spencer jumped on a plane to New Zealand to meet the receivers at the head office of Pumpkin Patch. Within a few hours, we'd bought the worldwide rights for the Pumpkin Patch brand. Why did we do this? Good question. We asked ourselves the same question seven months later when it all went to shit, but like all our endeavours, it seemed like a good idea at the time.

Looking back, it's clear we were a little blinded by the brand. It was iconic and we wanted to own it. It did come with a huge database of mostly female shoppers of all age groups who were highly aligned with the Catch customer demographic. We saw value in that. We figured we had been selling fashion for years and so running a fashion label couldn't be that much harder to do and it would allow us to have our own private label of clothes without starting a brand from scratch. We were perhaps riding high on the thrill of our recent successes and believed we had the Midas touch and that everything we touched would turn to gold. We also suffered from the syndrome we had so carefully cultivated in our customers at Catch: FOMO. Pumpkin Patch seemed like a good deal and we didn't want to miss out on it. After all, we are great buyers, aren't we?

Focus on what you know

There's a saying in business and life: stick to what you know best. When it came to Pumpkin Patch, maybe we should have. The mistake we made was we didn't truly understand what it takes to run a fashion label and the complexities in the supply chain that underpinned it. Being apparel, it involved choosing designs that resonated with the target market, seasonality, demand forecasting and commitment to huge volumes of stock in a variety of combinations (colours, sizes, styles), fast-moving tastes, not to mention photographic sessions featuring temperamental kids, their mums, casting agents and the like. No offence, we love kids—we have six of them between us—but we live for speed and once you introduce crying babies and all these other variables things slow down in a big way.

Long story short, we spent a few months building the site, and hired designers, buyers, managers and marketers to run it. But for a range of reasons, it just didn't work. We were disappointed.

If changing your mind is a sign of intelligence, we were Einsteins. The brand was perhaps more suited to someone with the right infrastructure and experience. That wasn't us. Seven months after buying Pumpkin Patch, we sold it to a New Zealand based company called EziBuy. A perfect home for a great brand.

While we considered the Pumpkin Patch foray to be a big failure, we also believed that you can learn a lot from your failures and we have always encouraged our people to take risks. While we both loathe failing at anything, we loathe lack of initiative even more. The lesson? Sometimes you win, sometimes you lose. But if you lose, decide quickly and move on.

Learning from the masters

The Catch marketplace was on fire and we were thrilled that an idea we had been incubating as a conversation for many years had finally flowered and borne fruit. It was exciting to see our new logo out in the world and know that we were competing with global brands such as Amazon and eBay and holding our own.

But we were never content to sit back and relax. We were always keen to experiment, stretch ourselves and challenge our team to see what we could accomplish. So, when two of our most loyal employees, Anees and Vijay, came to us with an idea to grow the market further we couldn't resist the opportunity. The idea? To inspire our customers to pre-pay their shipping fees for a whole year.

WTF? What customer in their right mind would do that?

As it turns out, 200 000 of them—and the number is growing daily.

While the idea of asking customers to pre-pay their shipping fees was new to many Australian e-commerce companies, it wasn't new to our arch competitor, Amazon. They had yet to arrive in Australia, or take a foothold, so we figured now was a good time to replicate one of their masterstrokes of marketing and try it at Catch. Their 'Prime' membership program had been wildly successful for them and we thought it could be equally powerful for us. You don't need to be original to succeed!

Costco had done it successfully for many years and while they gave their customers very little back for the membership fee (other than some good deals) we resolved to give our customers such great value, they would be lining up to pay it. And that's exactly what happened.

Anees and Vijay were the architects of what became known as Club Catch. (We were very proud of that name too. It has served us well for many years. Never forget—a great name will be your greatest asset!) For $69 per year, our customers received free shipping on orders of $45 or more within a 12-month period, and they could purchase as many times as they liked. The results were spectacular! We found that customers who used to buy from us three times a year increased their purchasing with us to as much as 10 times a year! This proved three things: our customers loved us, they trusted us and they wanted to buy more from us. We just needed to give them a good reason to do so, and Club Catch was it.

Club Catch wasn't just a superb tool for building loyalty and creating an unexpected source of cash flow. It became a valuable tool in our arsenal of ammunition and was integral to Wesfarmers acquiring us in 2019. After the deal, both Kmart and Target invited their customers to join Club Catch, demonstrating yet again how a little start-up could teach a global retailer a thing or two.

P.S. Want free shipping from Kmart, Target and Catch? Go ahead! Join Club Catch today and get it. Yes, we're always selling. We can't help ourselves. It's in our DNA.

P.P.S. Anees and Vijay eventually left Catch after 10 years of loyal service. We couldn't have done what we did without them.

It's complicated

Bon Voyage was travelling well and annoying the crap out of the market leader Luxury Escapes. So much so that just five months after we launched the site, we managed to sign and agree on terms for a most complicated deal with the Lux Group. This *Travel Trends* article by Martin Kelly sums it up best.

The Lux Group, which owns online travel business Luxury Escapes, has bought Scoopon Travel and BonVoyage as part of a complicated, multi-faceted transaction with the Catch Group that will create a pure-play online travel business with $300m turnover and enormous buying power while clearing the way for further growth.

In what the companies are calling Australia's largest "home grown" e-commerce transaction, the deal sees the Lux Group essentially divest all its non-travel assets to Catch Group, while welcoming Catch Group founders, Gabby and Hezi Leibovich, on board as 20% shareholders.

For Catch Group, the reverse applies.

The rationale is that the deal allows each company to play to their strengths. In a series of related transactions:

- Catch Group is buying Brands Exclusive and Thehome. com.au from Lux Group.

- Lux Group brands Cudo, Living Social and TreatMe (NZ) will merge with Catch Group deals business Scoopon.

- Lux Group and Catch Group are forming a new 50/50 'Local Experience' joint venture.

Lux Group Managing Director Adam Schwab said it was a transformative transaction for both parties.

"It was an obvious thing to do – we wanted to become a travel business and focus on our core strengths.

"This transformative transaction will allow Lux Group to establish a focussed and scaled Travel ecommerce business with over A$300m of pro forma turnover as we continue to deliver the world's very best travel packages to consumers across Australia, New Zealand and South East Asia."

...Catch Group co-founder Gabby Leibovich said the deal makes a lot of sense.

> "Our strength is in sourcing products and we have mastered the logistics of ecommerce," he said.
>
> "With Catch Group's travel brands on track to turn over more than $50 million this year, and product brands at Lux Group heading towards $60 million in turnover, we are very excited to partner with Lux and to be able to build on our respective strengths together to continue to grow and dominate Australia's ecommerce landscape."

So much achieved in such a short space of time. Within 15 months we had managed to:

- ✓ buy back our share of the business from Tiger and the consortium
- ✓ parachute a new CEO into Catch and change almost the entire management team
- ✓ rebrand Catchoftheday to Catch.com.au
- ✓ launch a dedicated luxury travel brand, Bon Voyage
- ✓ launch a marketplace that allowed us to increase our product range from fewer than 30 000 products to more than 2 million products
- ✓ launch Pumpkin Patch
- ✓ launch a New Zealand website, Catch.co.nz
- ✓ merge Scoopon with Cudo and LivingSocial into a 50/50 entity
- ✓ sell Bon Voyage for an equity stake in Luxury Escapes
- ✓ purchase two retail sites from Lux Group: Thehome.com.au and brandsexclusive.com.au
- ✓ receive 20 per cent of Luxury Escapes.

Ahhh, we forgot one. We also launched Catch Connect, a joint venture with Optus offering mobile phone plans to the Catch audience.

All up, not a bad financial year for 2017. After our 'Year of Nothing' in 2016, we called this our 'Year of Everything'.

These mergers had a massive impact on our operations, both financially and culturally. We felt like we'd jettisoned some dead weight and removed some weaknesses and distractions, which freed us up to move quickly and more profitably. The result? We kick-started FY2018 with a laser-sharp focus: sell more products and turn Catch.com.au into the biggest business possible. The boat was much lighter, the sails were up, the wind was blowing and we were flying.

Amazon (finally) arrives

While the marketplace had been a huge success, the race was on. The media had been breathlessly reporting for months that Amazon was coming. It seemed every story they ran had to include a reference to Amazon. While Amazon wasn't the first mover in Australia, it sure as heck felt like it. Everyone was in thrall to the monster that Amazon was promising to be. We just wished they would arrive so we could get on with beating them. You can't fight an invisible threat.

Finally, just five months after we launched the Catch marketplace, Amazon launched in Australia. The impact was felt instantly. Like a domino piece, it set off a chain reaction in the industry and forced every retailer in the country to rethink their business model, including us. eBay pulled their finger out and went on a massive advertising campaign. JB Hi-Fi and others like them made strong moves to improve their logistics offering, and Amazon was discussed at every boardroom meeting around the country.

David vs Goliath

We grew up watching Bruce Lee movies and loved it when little Bruce managed to beat 20 big guys against all the odds. We identified with Bruce because we've always felt we were the David in our very own Goliath story. For example, when we launched Scoopon in 2010, we went up against a market goliath in Groupon. They entered the market with buckets full of marketing dollars and were here to win. It happened when we launched Grocery Run, with Coles and Woolworths firmly in our sights. In 2017, we did it again, staring down the likes of eBay and the imminent arrival of Amazon as we launched the Catch marketplace.

On each of these occasions, few in the market or media gave us a chance of succeeding. But they didn't know us, or know what we were capable of. We may not have been bigger or stronger, but we were smarter and faster. Here are two strategies we used to outmanoeuvre the big players.

Think differently

If you're going to disrupt a legacy industry, you need to identify what makes your business unique and build on that. Thinking differently, creating a strong point of differentiation and creating a buzz around our edgy brand was our key to success. Our marketing was strong, consistent, bold and it cut through. Aldi has done the same. Their tagline of 'Good. Different' and their out-of-the-box advertising campaigns positioned them as a real alternative to the seemingly impenetrable Goliaths of Coles and Woolworths.

Be agile

David is fast and agile. Goliath is bloated and cumbersome. Goliath has to wait for the monthly board meeting in order to get approval for a major decision. David makes water-cooler decisions and as such can get to the finish line much more quickly. David wins the war by the time Goliath wakes up from his winter sleep. If you're a start-up and you don't have deep pockets, you need to be more like David. We made a point of outlasting, outsmarting and outplaying the Goliaths in our sectors and we came out on top. We've always identified with David and, to be honest, we don't think we would have had as much fun being Goliath.

By sheer coincidence or pure genius (we think the latter!) the timing of our marketplace launch was impeccable. You see, by the time Amazon launched in Australia, our marketplace was already up and running, and was host to hundreds of happy sellers and millions of even happier buyers.

Our sellers loved the fact we could deliver them a huge audience of hungry buyers and our customers loved that we could offer them a huge range of products at the best prices. Our business model was sound; our transactional capabilities were first rate; our automated warehouse was firing on all cylinders; and we had the best, most experienced e-commerce management team in the country.

By launching early, we established ourselves as a force to be reckoned with. When the media talked about the three main marketplaces in Australia, Catch was listed alongside eBay and Amazon as a leading player.

This was a 'pinch me' moment. Our home-made e-commerce site was being compared and contrasted alongside the global Leviathans of online business, Amazon and eBay, each worth a thousand billion trillion dollars! (Is there such a number?)

We spent the rest of FY2018 building on the success of the marketplace, and by year end the marketplace offering added $65 million of sales to our overall revenue, and more than 40 per cent of our daily orders were generated by our marketplace sellers, which was well ahead of any of our most optimistic projections! Our total sales for the 2018 financial year were $321 million, which was 65 per cent more than our 2017 product revenue. These results, according to the *Australian Financial Review* (AFR), placed us at the top of the pyramid as Australia's highest selling pure play e-commerce site. We couldn't have been happier.

Joining Luxury escapes with Cameron Holland (L) and Adam Schwab (R).
Source: **Photo by Josh Robenstone**

CHAPTER 16

To list, or not to list: that is the question

In addition to revitalising our retail and marketplace offerings, we spent the year preparing to list on the Australian Stock Exchange. Listing is a major endeavour and not a road you go down without the best of the best advising you.

To that end, we engaged the services of Intrinsic Partners, a corporate advisory firm, and our legal team at SBA Law to assist with the endeavour. The team at Intrinsic Partners (including founder Quentin Miller, Jason Bagg and Ronan Fenton) undertook and guided us through an incredible amount of work and preparation for the transaction. In fact, the preparation actually commenced in 2017 when Intrinsic Partners advised Catch on a complex restructuring of the business that involved asset swaps and a joint venture with Luxury Escapes. Importantly, this resulted in Catch becoming a pure play product business, which would be more readily understood by potential acquirers and the investment market.

Quentin Miller

Our brief was to help the Catch team become 'investor ready' and to project manage the IPO (initial public offering) process. We spent many months working with their management team to help translate what they do at Catch into a language the investors and financial markets would understand.

When you work as closely in the business as they did, it's hard to see the forest for the trees. We helped them step back and identify the basic building blocks of what made Catch so profitable and why an investor would want to invest in them.

After many discussions, we distilled their 13 years of business history into a concise, investor-friendly document that we could show to potential board members and Joint Lead Managers (JLMs) who would be coming on this IPO journey with them.

We issued a Request for Proposal to appoint JLMs and received a number of submissions*. The stand-out applications were from UBS and Canaccord Genuity, and after much negotiation and discussion we appointed the latter as partners in the process, and soon after that, PwC were selected as the independent accountants. We undertook an equally rigorous process with appointing board members and after meeting with 20 high calibre individuals, chose Gary Levin as the chair.

Our next step was to establish a Due Diligence Committee (DDC). This was a key part of the IPO process and required input from the management team, all the advisers and the board members to meet bi-weekly and scrutinise the business in minute detail, including the current trading results, forecasts and IPO documents.

Once all the documentation was in place, we kicked off the investor process with what's known as a 'non-deal roadshow'. If the guys were rock stars, this would be their stadium tour. Preparing for it was arduous. With our assistance, Nati, Mark

---

* Sorry, we know this is boring, but we thought it might be of interest to those start-ups out there looking to list. We hope our experience can be of value to you. Listing is not for the faint-hearted. Choose your advisory team carefully.

Spencer (the CFO), Adam Kron, Gabby and Hezi created a presentation pack and spent days rehearsing their roles so they could deliver it with confidence. They even hired a presentation coach to help them get it right and to throw tough questions at them so they'd be well trained to deal with any curly questions that came their way.

Around the world in seven days

 Gabby

We set off on our international roadshow, which sounds like fun though it was anything but. We travelled to Melbourne, Sydney, Auckland and Hong Kong to woo the investment community. I am no stranger to hard work, but this was one of the hardest weeks of my life. It's a common joke in financial circles that once you've done one roadshow, you'll never do another ever again.

It's not a joke. It's a fact. It was arduous.

Picture this: 70 meetings in three countries over seven days (that's 10 meetings a day!) saying pretty much the same thing, like a parrot, hour after hour, and still trying to stay excited about the whole thing. I was so hyped at the start of the roadshow that I went shopping and bought a fancy suit and tie for the week ahead. I started strong and wore my nicely ironed outfit on day one and day two, but by day three I'd had enough and just went to the meetings unshaven and dressed in jeans and my black T-shirt with a big Catch logo. I was past the point of trying to impress. I just wanted it to be over.

When we got back to Australia, the work continued. We went straight back into the meeting room with our advisers to finalise our forecast financials, create a prospectus and prepare for the analyst briefings. But it was all for naught.

We were knackered: 70 meetings, 3 countries, 10 days. In Hong Kong: Adam Kron, Mark Spencer, Nati, Gabby.

No listing for us.

In the first week of September 2018, nearly a full year after we started preparing for the IPO, we received a phone call from our advisers. The message? The world economy was in flux, the markets were choppy and investors had fled the market. This was not a good time to be listing. The call was met with mixed emotions.

On one hand we were disappointed. We had put so much into it, had spent hundreds of hours preparing for it and were excited to see how far we could take the company. On the other hand, we were secretly pleased the decision to not list had been taken out of our hands.

Hezi said it best.

Hezi

The truth was that as founders we never really wanted to be at the helm of a publicly listed company.

You've probably guessed by now we're not corporate types and we don't always do things in the boring, corporate way, so you can imagine how we'd bristle at the scrutiny and glacial pace of decision making that occurs within a public company.

It's common to see companies having to make decisions to please a range of stakeholders such as analysts, who sometimes don't even have the customers' interests (or that of the business) at heart, as opposed to making the decisions that are the best for the business at that point in time.

We never wanted to play that game. If the deal had gone through, we'd be a listed company by now, and our market capitalisation could have been even greater than our eventual sale price to Wesfarmers. But Gabby and I were clear from the get-go about our intentions for being in business. Neither of us wanted to be the richest people in the cemetery, and we certainly didn't want to be 80-year-old men running a retail company and doing the same thing we'd been doing for the previous 50 years. So, all things considered, when we got that phone call, we felt a huge sigh of relief. It meant we could live another day without all the bullshit associated with a potential listing. As we write this book, we have discussed this scenario again, and with the benefit of hindsight, we are still sure we made the correct choice.

Just say 'yes' and work the rest out later

Not long after we got the phone call to advise us the IPO was cancelled, we received another phone call that opened up an unexpected opportunity, one much more to our liking. It was from Chadstone Shopping Centre in Melbourne, Australia's largest and busiest shopping centre. The news?

> *Toys R Us has gone bust. Christmas is around the corner. We have a very large empty space available for four months only, and we want Catch in it.*

Nati remembers taking the phone call and thinking, 'No way! We are too busy! We've got a million things going on. It's Christmas. We're at capacity, and we're not set up to be a bricks and mortar retailer.' But, as a well-known entrepreneur is renowned for saying, 'Screw it! Let's do it!'

The time frames were tight. Few companies could harness the troops as quickly as we did to bring the opportunity to life, but moving quickly is in our DNA. It was all hands on deck, including the management team. We hadn't worked in bricks and mortar since our Springvale store got flooded more than a decade earlier, but our memories were vivid (how could we forget!) and we knew exactly what to do and how to do it. A cavalcade of activities needed to take place, each at the right time and in the right order. We needed to organise the store design and fit-out, create store signage, order plastic bags, set up credit card facilities, install cash registers, print pricing tickets, schedule staffing rosters, book the print ads, amend the website, coordinate the warehouse, stack the shelves, deliver the stock. It was a whole-of-office endeavour and everyone rose to the occasion. And of course, everything was done on a shoestring budget! Russell Proud, our head of operations, took care of IT and integration while Ivan, our head of customer service, had his work cut out for him. He hired a whole new team of shop assistants and trained them to uphold and deliver the high standards our Catch customers had come to know and expect.

Within 30 days, we had transformed a 2000 m² area into a Christmas-themed, Catch-branded store showcasing the best that Catch had to offer. Toys, homewares, apparel, shoes, appliances— all the top brands at Australia's best prices.

As always, we turned on the PR machine, cranked up the volume and watched the stories roll out. We secured prime time coverage on all the news and current affairs TV shows, and scored acres of newsprint in the daily newspapers. That coverage, coupled with our own campaigns, drove unprecedented levels of foot traffic not only to our store, but also to Chadstone Shopping Centre itself. We couldn't believe the response. Our shop, just a few days old, had lines forming outside that snaked down the side of the store and beyond. At one stage, on Christmas Eve, it got so busy we had to hire security guards (including Gabby, Hezi and Nati) to block the entrance because the queues were getting out of control. It was a frenzy of activity, but we loved every second of it.

We were particularly stoked to see that our recipe for success was working offline now, as well as online. Our long-standing online customers could now come in-store, meet us in person and say hello to the team who had been loyally serving them for so long. And conversely, customers who discovered us in-person at Chadstone for the first time could jump on our website and see the breadth and depth of what we offered online. Our suppliers loved it as it gave them the opportunity to showcase their products to a new audience. Our management team, who all put their hands up to staff the store for a shift or two, got to hear real feedback in real time from our customers, which further informed the way the team went about their work. We've always been about getting close to the customer and now we literally were.

The Catch store at Chadstone. We had to hire security guards to keep the crowds under control.

The entire experience was a win-win-win situation for all, and priceless on so many levels. Not only did it prove that we could accomplish almost any retail challenge we set our minds to, and do so in record time, it proved that we could match any bricks and mortar retailer and show them how retail is really done.

Mission accomplished

While the Chadstone store was generating record sales, our online sales were also going through the roof. November is the busiest month of the year for retailers and this year was no different. We were sending out 20 000 orders every day to our ever-growing customer base. Seeing the business turn around after those few years of plateauing gave us all enormous gratification. Our hard work, clarity of focus and appetite for risk had seen our graphs skyrocket in the right direction. One of the most important graphs we paid attention to was the one that counted the number of unique customers who had shopped with us over the previous 12-month period. Retailers worth their salt pay attention to this metric. It's the one that matters as it's an accurate and reliable measure of growth.

When we stepped back into the business, the unique number of customers who were shopping with us was 750 000. Eighteen months later, the number had doubled to 1.5 million unique customers. An incredible result, and a product of the many major (and minor) decisions we had made over the period. This was an important metric for us because it showed that people kept coming back to us and were telling their friends and family about us too. If people aren't happy, they don't come back, and if that number is going down, it's the canary in the coalmine for any online business. But people loved shopping with us and came back time and time again. We had the numbers to prove it.

We celebrated our thirteenth birthday, our bar-mitzvah year, with a big party, lots of great food, drinks and music and many toasts to our team for the part they had played in bringing Catch back from the brink. It's just as well we celebrated long and hard into the night that year because little did we know that birthday celebration was to be our last with Catch. A week after celebrating the event, we received another approach, this time via email, that would change our lives forever.

CHAPTER 17

Wesfarmers come calling

Wesfarmers is one of Australia's largest listed companies. It started as a farmers' cooperative back in 1914 and now is a diversified conglomerate worth over $50 billion, with retail operations that include blue-chip operations such as Bunnings, Kmart, Target and Officeworks. You could say they know retail.

So, imagine our surprise when we strolled into work one morning to find an email from the heads of Wesfarmers sitting in our inbox. The subject line? 'Catch up?' There were other lines in that email that caught our eye. 'Comparing notes on ways we can work together' and 'A marketplace offer is an obvious hole in our strategy'.

Our first reaction?

Holy shit! Is this what we think it is? Is Wesfarmers, this monolith of Australia's greatest brands, courting us? It is and they were. Could our Fair-Etail get any better?

Here's what happened.

Gabby

The meeting with Wesfarmers took place at the offices of Intrinsic, our financial advisers, in Cremorne, an inner-city suburb of Melbourne. We had no idea what to expect. We took our seats at the boardroom table, and watched as the top brass from Wesfarmers filed in. After the initial introductions were over, their most senior representative took to the stage to express his admiration for what we at Catch stood for, for what we had achieved and for how we'd done it. This 'love fest' went on for a full 45 minutes and, to be honest, I loved every minute of it.

I had a million thoughts running through my mind, but the one I found hardest to comprehend was that Australia's most respected retailer could be so freely congratulatory to these two schmucks. We'd always been the outsiders and now, here we were being courted by a company that represented the establishment.

When it came time for me to respond, I managed to get out a couple of coherent sentences and then…I burst out crying! I couldn't help it. I was so overwhelmed with emotion at what I was hearing, and the honesty and sincerity with which it had been delivered. It was embarrassing but at the same time, it was me! I've always worn my heart on my sleeve. I don't pretend to be anyone I'm not, or pretend to know more than the next guy. That emotional response was me reacting to the 13 years of risk-taking, back-breaking work we had put in to build this business from scratch. And now, here we were, with the crème de la crème of corporate Australia courting us. It was an introductory meeting but they could not have been more open, sincere and direct. They loved what they saw and they weren't afraid to say it. After much hand shaking (and hugging—what can I say? I'm a hugger!) we parted ways with a commitment to follow up in the next week.

I wiped my eyes, blew my nose and said to Hezi, 'It was a good meeting' [more crying]. 'I think this deal is going ahead.'

Surround yourself with the best advisers

Our first financial adviser was from a medium-tier firm. He filled in the paperwork, balanced the books, paid our tax and all that stuff. We had no complaints and we didn't know any differently. Being new in business, we did not yet understand the importance and value of finding the right adviser. Over the previous 12 years our business had been cradled in the safe hands of Guy Biran from JM Partners. Guy is so much more than an accountant. He's a guide, a confidant and truly a third partner in our business journey. We could not have done what we've done without him. Thank you, buddy!

Furthermore, as you get bigger, you'll want to surround yourself with other helpful advisers, including a good lawyer. Good advice from skilled professionals doesn't come cheap, but those people are worth their weight in gold. Our advisers helped us get investment from Tiger, sell Menulog, merge with Luxury Escapes, sell Catch to Wesfarmers, and much more. So we'd also like to thank Joe Zhao, Quentin Miller, Jason Bagg, Ronan Fenton, Steven Klein, Joshua Heard, Paul Thorpe-Apps, Jeremy Goldman and all the advisers from Goldman Sachs, KPMG, UBS, Macquarie, PwC and many others who supported us on our journey.

How do you find your team of advisers? Don't go with that friend of a friend who lives next door to your cousin. Do your research, ask around, look to LinkedIn and find the best within your budget. Quick tip: Don't take advice from people who don't understand your business. Choose wisely.

Signing the Wesfarmers deal. Choose your advisers carefully. Standing, from left to right: Jason Bagg, Steven Klein, Hezi, Ronan Fenton, Nati, Guy Biran, Quentin Miller. Seated: Joshua Heard, Gabby.

The Midas touch

The due diligence process that took place was...diligent...as you would expect from a company this size, but what worked in our favour was that because we had done the groundwork for the IPO a few months earlier, our financials, prospectus and roadmap were already in order. That marathon roadshow of meetings we attended a year earlier prepped us perfectly for the barrage of discussions that would take place before this deal could be consummated.

The speed at which we delivered this due diligence demonstrated to Wesfarmers we were a company that had its act together. What else played in our favour was that we were a tremendously profitable company, we were growing at a rate of knots, and we were led by a super-motivated management team that was doing it better than almost any company in the sector.

Throughout the due diligence process, we made a point of not being present at the meetings or being part of the strategic conversations. We wanted to send a deliberate message to Wesfarmers (and our own team) that the founding brothers would not be continuing with the business and that it would be led by the CEO and the wider management team. Our rationale was, and has always been, that we hired smart people because they were smart, and that this was the moment to let them do what we had hired them to do: lead the company.

We, as the founders of the company, knew from the get-go that Wesfarmers would only be interested in buying 100 per cent of the business. The truth was, we would have loved to have kept a small slice of the business and continued supporting it in any way possible, but we just knew that this would not be acceptable to Wesfarmers.

People often ask why Wesfarmers took such an interest in our business. We've asked ourselves the same question, and after many discussions with them, the reasons became clear. They were impressed with our digital expertise, logistics capability, sustained profitability, the Catch marketplace and its ability to provide customers of Wesfarmers' retail businesses with an alternative to Amazon.

These were the tangibles that made us attractive, but there were some intangibles that made us equally appealing. When Ian Bailey, the Managing Director of Kmart and Target, addressed our warehouse team soon after the transaction, he put into words what many in the industry had grappled with—namely, why we had been successful when so many had not. He said:

> We have been observing Catch for a number of years now, and it feels like year after year you are advancing forward and building a stronger and stronger business. This is not an easy thing to do in such a competitive market and it is a great testament to the hard work, focus and innovation of the leadership and the team in Catch.

The other intangible reason that made us attractive as an acquisition was our extraordinary team and the intrapreneurial energy they brought to the business. They represented the culture that had made Catch so successful.

This acquisition deal was nine months in the making and involved hundreds of people at various levels of both corporations working closely to bring it to fruition. But interestingly, not one person from either team leaked the news to the media or the industry. We were able to conduct these protracted and complex negotiations in secret, which made it much easier for everyone involved to do the work that needed to be done. We think it's a testament to the teams on both sides that their loyalty trumped their temptation to leak what would be a very tasty morsel of industry gossip.

As we wander through the many Wesfarmers-owned companies that dominate the shopping malls of retail Australia we are heartened to see that they have implemented many of the marketing strategies that were innovated and incubated at Catch.

One of our proudest moments was walking into Melbourne's Highpoint Shopping Centre at Maribyrnong and seeing a Catch store-within-a-store right there inside Target. Our little online store that started in a garage was up in lights inside a shopping icon. *Surreal.* It's the only word that can truly describe how that feels.

CHAPTER 18

A final note: how to *really* succeed in business

We saved the best, and perhaps the most important, message for last. Why? Two reasons.

First, we wanted to reward those persistent few who stuck around and made it to the end of the book. (Did you know 87 per cent of people never finish reading a business book*?)

Second, it's the message that truly answers the question we started with in the beginning, which was, to paraphrase...

> *How do two schmucks with no money, no tech background and no contacts build some of Australia's most successful digital businesses?*

Having written the book, and spent months reconstructing the events of our lives that led us to where we are today, the answer is very simple.

It's All. About. The. People.

---

* Don't quote us on this. We have no idea if this figure is accurate or not.

Sure, there's a bunch of other reasons why we, and not others, were able to achieve so much when we started with so little. But the most important reason we succeeded is because of this: we surrounded ourselves with outstanding people, people who worked as if the business belonged to them.

This principle actually has a name. We didn't know that when we were running the business (we operated instinctively), but this principle of enabling a team to dare greatly and possibly fail in the process (and still celebrate their effort anyway) is called 'Intrapreneurship'. We talked about it earlier and only dedicated a page to it but, looking back over the years, we believe our ability to foster autonomy, independence and courage enabled us to create a fertile environment in which intrapreneurship could flourish, and it subsequently made Catch more successful than we could have ever imagined.

It's not a management style that suits everyone. You need humility to step aside and let the team do their thing. You need to let them take risks and challenge the status quo. You need to remove the hierarchies, create a 'flat' organisation and give the intrapreneurs the space to act like entrepreneurs.

But the effort is worth it because when you hire, build, encourage and empower intrapreneurs, and get out of their way, the results are exponentially more than the sum of the parts. You'll be free to concentrate on strategy, knowing the intrapreneurs will carry it out beyond your expectations. You won't have an egotistical, self-centred team of superstars working for their own interests. You'll have a superstar team, who all know their role and work towards a common goal … like Liverpool in 2020!

Throughout this book we shared many lessons and learnings that we have accumulated throughout the years, but it all comes down to this: no-one, but no-one can do everything on their own, so make sure you surround yourself with the right people who will treat the business as if it were their own, and together you can build on your dreams.

GOODBYE, FAREWELL AND GOOD LUCK

When we sat down to write our final email to say goodbye, farewell and good luck to those who had been a part of our journey for so long, we struggled to put into words what we were feeling. How do you say goodbye to a team, a business, a lifestyle that had defined who and what you are for more than a decade? What do you say to those who have helped you achieve your wildest dreams and given you back so much more than you could ever give them? It went something like this and it's a fitting end to our book.

It was early 2006, back in the early days of online shopping. eBay Australia had launched a year earlier, and few, if any, of the big retail players had launched their own website, let alone started selling online.

We decided to jump in, headfirst, and they laughed at us. 'Selling one product every single day? You must be crazy!' they said. 'Why would anyone come to a site that has only one product a day? That's not a business!'

We must have been mad to think that something like this would work, but by 2008 we had managed to sell 4000 Toshiba laptops in a single day and $1 million worth of Samsung TVs in an hour, just to name a couple of deals.

By 2010 Catch of the Day was Australia's No.1, the most visited shopping site. This achievement put us on the map and stirred up the retail landscape like never before.

The next few years have been busy to say the least. In no particular order, we launched, built or acquired:

- *Scoopon*
- *Grocery Run*
- *Mumgo*
- *Vinomofo*
- *Yumtable*
- *EatNow*
- *Pumpkin Patch*
- *Bon Voyage*
- *Thehome*
- *Brandsexclusive*
- *Catch marketplace.*

Over the past 13 years we've shared this journey with more than 1000 workmates. They are our friends who have become our family. We can't name you all but we thank each and every one of you from the bottom of our hearts for taking part in this incredible journey! We are so proud of everything that we achieved together and will treasure these friendships for the rest of our lives.

We believe that we have taken the business as far as we could, and to sail through the rough seas of retail, Catch needs new ownership and guidance. So, it's time to pass on the baton.

We are leaving Catch on a massive high! A strong Australian brand that is much loved, with a reputation that is second to none. Our team is the best in the country, and as such it was no surprise that an Australian retail leader, Wesfarmers, saw the opportunity to take Catch to places that we could not.

We remember back in the early days, going into Kmart Chadstone around midnight, to find inspiration. We flipped the products around, checking the labels in order to find new suppliers. ☺ And now, here we are, owned by that very same company.

We would like to use this opportunity to thank the team at Wesfarmers (you know who you are). You recognised that our brands shared a common DNA, and that's a great start for any union. We are so humbled and excited that our baby, now a teenager, is joining your esteemed family of companies. Your admiration for what we have achieved, your praise for the team behind the success and your vision for the future have left us humbled and honoured. You were bold enough to seize the opportunity and to recognise Catch as a crucial part of the Wesfarmers story.

We are handing over a great business, with an amazing following of dedicated customers who trust us with their hard-earned day after day. But most of all we trust you with our Catch family, the 400+ super smart, dedicated, hard-working people who love working together and punching above their weight. Please take care of them!

We would like to use this opportunity to thank our suppliers and service providers (again, too many to mention). Without them, we are nothing! Catch has built its reputation and success on the back of great deals. These deals are sourced from thousands of suppliers around the world. Thank you to each and every one of you for jumping on the Catch train and trusting us with your products. Some of you joined as early as 2006 (Telefunken, PowerDC, Lenoxx) and some of you have joined more recently (LG, Fila, Beats and many more).

The world of retail is changing, and you can no longer ignore the tidal wave. We know that with the change of ownership and having Wesfarmers behind Catch this will drive a massive influx of new and exciting brands and products to Catch. Our customers are going to love it!

Last but not least, the biggest thank you goes to our millions of customers. We know that you have a lot of choice out there, and yet you choose Catch, and that means the world to us. We hope that over the past decade or so we have managed to satisfy, surprise and delight you with great brands and great prices. We really have tried our best to do so. And you thanked us by coming back for more and more, telling your friends about us, and making it the massive site it is today.

Stick with Catch. We've got a good feeling that it is just the beginning and there are lots of great things in store. We've only just begun.

People like us never reach their destination as we always push the boundaries forward. We love solving problems, and problems will always be around. We are your friends forever, and have a lot of time for coffees or walks around the park. We will forever support this brand in any way that we can, so please feel free to reach out to us for advice, recommendations or just for a coffee.

So, it's goodbye and good luck from the two of us. Don't be a stranger. Connect with us on LinkedIn, check out our site at www.catchofthedecade.com and let us know what exciting, interesting ideas you've got going on. We're super interested in being part of the next wave of young entrepreneurship in Australia and beyond, and we've got some time on our hands, so get in touch!

Gabby and Hezi

P.S. 100% of our profits from this book go to www.good360.org and www.secondbite.org. Please support them if you can. They do great work.

Catches

1   If there are two founders and they always think alike, one of them is not necessary.

2   Two co-founders is better than one.

3   Two co-founders enable you to get a lot more done.

4   A solo founder will, by definition, always be the smartest person in the room.

5   Two people with contrasting opinions debating the merits of a decision almost always yields a better result.

6   A great partner is invigorated by your strengths, and compensates for your weaknesses.

7   You can build a start-up on your own, but it's easier and more fun doing it with someone else.

8   No one person has all the answers, but by collaborating with others, you have a better chance of finding the right one.

9   If you don't have a point of difference, you will struggle to beat the dominant player.

10   If your business is up for sale, lay low, keep an even keel and don't make any bombastic moves.

11   For every action (or inaction) there is an opposite reaction.

12	When you are absent from the minutia of running the business, you can lose control over the things that made it successful.
13	When you need to make change, do it quickly.
14	Document your corporate procedures so when staff leave, the knowledge doesn't leave with them.
15	No-one is irreplaceable.
16	Culture eats strategy for breakfast.
17	Strategy is important, but without a strong culture and a strong team, even the best strategy will fail.
18	The first thing a new CEO will do is bring change.
19	If you ask the people who work in the trenches what's wrong with the business, they will generally tell you. They'll also tell you how to fix it.
20	'Build the clock' so your team can make decisions independently of you.
21	Don't be afraid to change your mind. It's a sign you're flexible and open to new ideas.
22	If changing your mind is a sign of intelligence, be an Einstein.
23	When decisions get made on the basis of merit, rather than seniority, everyone wins.
24	If you want customers to be loyal, you need to give them a good reason to *be* loyal.
25	Don't underestimate the power of giving the team good coffee.
26	Retain a start-up mindset, even when you're not a start-up.
27	When in doubt, rely on your instinct.
28	If you want to grow, you'll need to take a gamble.

29	If you can't join them, beat them.
30	The solutions to problems are often close to home.
31	Marketplaces are eating the world.
32	Eighty per cent of entrepreneurial decisions are often made with 20 per cent visibility.
33	To secure your culture, you need to document your culture. Write it down and circulate it so everyone can see it. Enshrine it as part of your corporate DNA.
34	Don't make people wear suits to work. Stiff clothes crush creativity.
35	It's better to be in the game than watch from the sidelines.
36	If you're creating new logos or names, invite your staff to participate. They'll feel ownership over the process and be more willing to support the change.
37	Don't be elitist about where you sell your product. Be where the customer is.
38	New entrants to the sector can be a positive. A rising tide floats all boats.
39	Don't be afraid to be number two.
40	Don't chase a rabbit down a hole.
41	Focus on what you know.
42	Failing isn't great, but lack of initiative is worse.
43	Don't be content to sit back and relax. Always strive for more. Challenge yourself.
44	Being David is more fun than being Goliath.
45	If you want to outsmart the big players, you need to think differently and be agile.
46	Pay attention to the metrics. They matter.

47 Get the best lawyer you can afford.

48 Don't take advice from people who haven't seen success or don't understand your business. Choose your advisers wisely.

49 Hire people with an intrapreneurial nature, empower them to take risks and get out of their way.

50 For intrapreneurs to flourish, remove the hierarchy, create a 'flat' organisation and give them the space to act like entrepreneurs.

51 No-one can do everything on their own, so surround yourself with people who treat your business as if it were their own.

52 It's. All. About. The. People.

The gang!

ACKNOWLEDGEMENTS

Whenever we experienced a major milestone in the business, good or bad, Gabby would say, 'This one's for the book!', without every really knowing if there'd be a book.

Well, now there is, and fortunately, we've got a few photos to accompany it to help paint the picture of how we started and where we ended.

This book was written during COVID-19 and was released in November 2020. We wrote it during the lockdown, which gave us a lot of time to reflect on what we've done, what we've learned and who the key people were that helped us along the way.

We had a million stories to tell and tried our best to pick and choose the best ones that you would find interesting, or at least instructive. We had to cull many, and as much as we think there's room for a sequel (*Fifty Shades of Catch*, anyone?), we wanted to give you the highlights and the lowlights, and leave out the bits-in-between because it's the extremes that made our journey interesting.

We started with nothing; we ended with something. Money, yes, but more than that, we ended with friendships that have stood the test of time. Friendships that have been forged through the good times and the bad times. This is our opportunity to thank all those people: friends, workmates, suppliers, competitors and everyone else who accompanied us on this journey of a lifetime.

Firstly, we would like to express our sincere thanks and appreciation to Bernadette Schwerdt, our ghost-writer, for all her help in making this book possible. Thank you for sitting with us for hundreds of hours, for helping us sift through the 200 000+ words we've written over the years, and for guiding us through the writing and publishing process that enabled us to find our voice, shape the narrative, and craft the stories that make up this book.

We would also like to thank the team at Wiley for their belief and support in this project from the very start. Special thanks to Lucy Raymond, Chris Shorten, Sandra Balonyi, Ingrid Bond, Bronwyn Evans and the team at Wiley for believing in this project and enabling us to share our story with the world. Thanks, guys, for making us 'published authors'!

Thank you also to the following friends for helping us proofread the book: Ido Lefler, Lance Kalish, Paul Greenberg, and Adir Shifman; to Jason Toon for some great writing; to Sadya Liberow from Creativecorner.com.au for the front cover design; to Luke Honey for photography; and to Ramoncito Abella for banner design.

A big thank you once again to our thousands of suppliers and service providers. This business is built on your support.

Thank you also to the first group that believed and invested in us back in 2011: Lee Fixel, Jason Lenga, James Packer, Andrew and Paul Bassat and Glenn Poswell.

And thank you to Jin Wang for the great book website, and to Debbie McInnes from DMCPR Media for the great PR for the book.

We cannot emphasise enough the importance and value of balancing work life with your family life and friendship. We wish that our grandparents were here to see us now, and this book is dedicated to them in so many ways.

Thank you to our parents Aaron and Edith, and sister Einat, for a childhood that every kid dreams of in the streets of Nahariya, Israel, and for giving us the tools to succeed.

Thank you to our close friends who have been there for us through the ups and downs, and those times when we needed them most.

We would like to thank Guy Biran (again!!) and Joe Zhao from JM Partners; and a big thank you to Paul Thorpe Apps, Quentin Miller, and Jason Bagg from Intrinsic Partners, Steven Klein and Joshua Heard from SBA Law, Jeremy Goldman from KCL Law and Nick Sims from Goldman Sachs.

Most importantly, we'd like to thank those who are closest to us and who have made all of this possible: our wives, Amanda and Lina. There were so many shaky moments and sleepless nights when things could have gone the wrong way, but they stuck with us throughout the journey and have been towers of strength and support throughout. We cannot thank them enough.

We'd like to thank our children, the pride of our lives, Liron, Shira and Miri (Gabby's children) and Daniel, Liam and Meital (Hezi's children), for giving us the strength to fight on and surf the stormy waves of entrepreneurship. When times were tough and we questioned our purpose, we'd say to each other, 'We are doing this for our kids' and that alone gave us the strength to carry on. Some are old enough to remember the journey, while others are too young, and we hope that this book will help them understand the reasons why their fathers are who they are. Keep your minds open, and be kind always—do what you love, and love what you do, and the rest will fall into place. We love you all so much.

Our families have all experienced the high and lows of building the company, and have had to endure years of talking to husbands and fathers who were not really listening or were just preoccupied with building the next big thing. They deserve a gold medal for that!

We have loved every moment of creating this book and feel blessed to be in a position to write it. We truly hope that you have enjoyed it too, and take from it the knowledge and wisdom you need to create the business of your dreams.

Let's continue the conversation at **catchofthedecade.com.**

INDEX

CPSIA information can be obtained
at www.ICGtesting.com
Printed in the USA
LVHW030007281120
672878LV00002B/2